D1359789

AMERICAN DAGUERREIAN ART

AMERICAN DAGUERREIAN ART

Floyd and *Marion Rinhart*

DISTRIBUTED BY CROWN PUBLISHERS, INC.

Acknowledgments

WE WISH TO THANK THE OWNERS OR CUSTODIANS OF MANY DAGUERREOTYPE COLLECTIONS that were made available to us for study. Francis W. Dolloff, print department, Museum of Fine Arts, Boston, was especially helpful to us as was Beaumont Newhall, director of George Eastman House. The Metropolitan Museum of Art and the New-York Historical Society kindly brought out their fine collections of daguerreotypes for our viewing. We are also grateful to Dr. Louis Sipley, director of the American Museum of Photography for answering many questions about Philadelphia daguerreian artists.

Our research of thermoplastic daguerreotype cases was greatly furthered by Dr. Philip W. Bishop, chairman, Arts and Manufactures, Smithsonian Institution, Washington, D. C., who gave us the use of his notes on Scovill Manufacturing Company, Waterbury, Connecticut; Edward H. Davis, historian of Scovill Manufacturing Company; and Rawson W. Haddon, director, Mattatuck Historial Society, Waterbury, Connecticut.

We are deeply indebted to Miss Josephine Cobb, specialist of iconography, National Archives, Washington, D. C., for her many valuable recommendations which aided our research for this volume.

In our search for identification of daguerreian scenes, we are indebted to Miss Stella Scheckter, reference librarian, New Hampshire State Library, Concord, New Hampshire, who furnished a clue to the Lebanon, New Hampshire, scene used in this volume; and to Sam Stevens, town historian, Lebanon, New Hampshire, who positively identified the street scene from a newspaper clipping in his collection. The gold-mining scene was identified through the help of James de T. Abajian, librarian, California Historical Society, and Ruth Ann Newport, curator, Tuolumne County Museum, Sonora, California, who helped us establish the scene as Jamestown, California.

The Frick Art Reference Library was most cooperative in trying to identify unknown photographs of paintings. In this regard, we are also grateful to Dr. David H. Wallace, curator, Independence National Historical Park, Philadelphia, Pennsylvania. We wish to thank Dr. Richard Wunder, curator, American Paintings, Museum of Fine Arts, Smithsonian Institution, Washington, D. C., for his help in the selection of portrait and scene comparisons for this volume.

Mrs. Dorothy Ross, Deerfield Beach, Florida, and George G. Hutchinson, chairman, division of English, Mills College of Education, New York City, have given us valuable aid in the editing of our manuscript and offered many welcome suggestions. We would like to acknowledge the assistance given us by Henri Davis, a master of photography, without whose initial teachings the reproduction copies in this book would not be possible.

LIBRARY OF CONGRESS CATALOG CARD NUMBER: 67–16521
PRINTED IN THE UNITED STATES OF AMERICA

Contents

List of Illustrations

Introduction

In writing this volume, it is our hope to dispel the common notion of many Americans that early pioneers of photography were mostly untrained itinerants who went about the country taking photographs with little or no thought to traditional art principles of style, proportion, posing, or lighting. Actually, the creations of many of these early pioneers, on thin silvered sheets of copper, were a distinct art craft.

After a continuing study over a period of years of the now remaining examples of the art of the daguerreians and thorough research of the social history of 1840–1860, we realized that here was an art craft that lacked widespread recognition and understanding; the profound influence exerted by the relatively short-lived daguerreian era, both on contemporary arts and social life of the American people, has never been fully explored. Only by viewing the work of many daguerreian artists can this art hope to be defined and a judgment made in proper perspective. After defining the worth of the daguerreian art in its entirety, it is important then to study each unique creation for its own merit.

The new art form began with the introduction of Daguerre's process to America in 1839. The American pioneers of the camera established a native school of art and by 1840 called themselves daguerreian artists; their creations were termed daguerreian art (sometimes spelled daguerrean, daguerrian).

Although it is true that many men from all walks of life thronged to the new art after its advent in America, the fall of 1839, most of those unsuitable to the profession quickly fell by the wayside after learning from bitter experience that to become a successful daguerreian entailed more than mere mechanical rote; it required a bit of artistic genius, a thorough knowledge of chemistry, and a generous amount of taste to produce fine daguerreotypes. The many successful daguerreian artists, especially in the larger cities and towns, were more often than not well-educated, sophisticated men. Many had traveled abroad; some had studied art or were already painters, engravers, or lithographers who were wholly aware of traditional art principles.

The question has been asked where pioneer daguerreians saw the works of art we claim influenced the daguerreian art of the era. From 1840 onward, art unions were established in almost all major American cities including New York, Philadelphia, Boston, Newark, Cincinnati, and Chicago. They were organized in the form of lotteries or raffles similar to that of the Irish Sweepstakes, and tickets went into every state and territory.

Each member subscribed five dollars a year, and in return received engravings of some of the many original paintings which had been bought by the unions from subscription money. At the end of the year, lucky winners at a drawing would receive the original paintings. In Chicago, in 1845, a Daguerreotype Art Union and Photographic Association was in existence which provided an opportunity for those who wished to own examples of daguerreian art. In New York City in 1849 Williams and Company, dealers in engravings, joined with other companies in setting up an International Art Union. Although a court injunction eventually sounded a death knell for many American art unions, its influence during this era did bring art to the masses and stimulated public interest. In addition to the influence of art unions, exhibitions of original paintings by American and European artists were commonplace in the larger towns and cities. Also the panorama, large original paintings in sections, used to illustrate lectures, brought art representations to areas all over America. Publications during this period illustrated engravings and lithographs.

As with primitive painting, the daguerreian art had for its roots the craftsmanship growing out of American eighteenth-century craft traditions. The daguerreotype, unlike primitive painting, was exact and precise in the portrayal of its subject. If the physical material used by the primitive painter and the daguerreian differed, often their approach to capture a subject was similar. Each, according to his individual ability and craftsmanship, had his own style. The daguerreian artist's subject treatment and technique also incorporated a delightful mixture of many traditional schools of painting, classicism as well as native art traditions.

When the daguerreian era drew to a close, the intermingling and intermixing of the painters of the brush and the adherents to the camera also drew to a close; each school went its separate way, each followed its individual talents. To mark the passing of the daguerreian era, many daguerreian artists wore black armbands in the mid-1850's. The daguerreotype had given way to cheaper forms of photography.

The photographs we have selected for this volume are the work of daguerreian artists, both known and unknown, during the period 1840–1860. Although most of the photographs are from daguerreotypes, a few ambrotypes (photographs on glass) are included because of the overlapping span of the daguerreian era. Selections were made on the basis of character portrayal, pose, color tone, and background technique. Comparisons of paintings and daguerreotypes in this book are intended to show a possible influence of daguerreian art on artists and the influence of existing art, both before and during the period of 1840–1860, on the daguerreians.

1

The Daguerreian Art and Portraiture

THE LONG ESTABLISHED ART OF PORTRAITURE BECAME INTERTWINED IN 1840 WITH A NEW art vehicle, the daguerreotype, an exact image reflected on a silvered sheet of copper, produced through the medium of the camera obscura. The photographic process, a result of experiments of Louis Daguerre and a fellow Frenchman Nicéphore Niépce, was first introduced in America in the fall of 1839; the art quickly took root and before a decade had passed some of the finest portraiture on silver in the world had been created.

The first American to foster the interaction of the old and the new art was Samuel F. B. Morse, a perceiving man of science, an inventor, and a portrait artist of distinction. Morse spoke of the daguerreotype's role in art and its influence before an annual supper of the National Academy of Design on April 24, 1840:

> The daguerreotype is undoubtedly destined to produce a great revolution in art, and we, as artists, should be aware of it and rightly understand its influence. This influence, both on ourselves and the public generally, will, I think, be in the highest degree favorable to the character of art. . . . Its influence on the artist must be great. By a simple and easily portable apparatus, he can now furnish his studio with fac-simile sketches of nature, landscapes, buildings, groups of figures, etc., scenes selected in accordance with his own peculiarities of taste; but not, as heretofore, subjected to his imperfect, sketchy translation into crayon or Indian ink drawings, and occupying days, and even weeks, in their execution; but painted by nature's self with a minuteness of detail. . . . To the architect it offers the means of collecting the finest production of modern architecture, with their proportion and details of ornament, executed in a space of time, and with an exactness.[1]

At the time of Morse's speech, April, 1840, portraiture on a daguerreotype plate was still in experimental development. During the spring of 1839, Morse had visited with Daguerre in Paris and had viewed some of the images reflected upon Daguerre's silvered plates. They had discussed the possibility of taking portraits from life, but Daguerre was skeptical as to its practicability because of the length of time the subject must remain "unmovable." The time required for taking a scene at that date was from fifteen to twenty minutes.

However, it was with portraiture that the new daguerreian art would excel, especially in America. Samuel Morse's background in portrait painting had made him visualize from the very beginning of the new art medium the likelihood of its use for portraiture. When the first booklets of Daguerre's photographic process arrived in America in September, 1839,

Morse began experimenting at once. He soon enlisted the help of John W. Draper, professor of chemistry of the City of New York University, who was also experimenting with the process on his own. Working together and apart, the men gradually made improvements until they were able to take a clear portrait. Draper, especially, realized the importance of chemicals, focus, lens, and length of camera box in relation to one another. These early attempts by Morse and Draper were conducted in a studio of glass on a rooftop of New York University in the early part of 1840. During this same period, after the arrival of Daguerre's manual, there were pioneers in other American cities who were conducting tests and improving the basic daguerreotype process. Other men who worked together were John Johnson and Alexander S. Wolcott. Wolcott, an instrument maker and manufacturer of dental supplies, was familiar with optics. He conceived the idea of using a concave reflector of rather large diameter and short focus. With this device, he was able to get fairly successful portraits about two and a half by two inches. Wolcott secured the first of many important photographic patents which would improve photography in America; it was dated May 8, 1840.[2] His method had the advantage of a much shorter exposure. Johnson and Wolcott also employed a method of illumination using filtered light screened by the use of bottles filled with blue vitriol to protect the sitter's eyes against the intense glare caused by the mirrored light reflection. Another improvement by early experimenters was the use of a galvanic battery to resilver defective or poorly silvered copperplates.[3] A good quality and highly polished surface was of utmost importance in obtaining a satisfactory portrait. Once the technical and chemical complexity of the new process was mastered and improved, portraiture became a reality. Time exposure by the fall of 1840 had been cut from minutes to seconds.[4] By 1841, as a result of the experiments of these early pioneers, rooftop and open sunlight photographs had almost completely given way to the indoor portrait, using skylights as a source of light.

Although Samuel Morse had emphasized the usefulness of the daguerreotype as an aid to fellow artists, his greatest influence in the beginning days of the infant art, when portraiture was becoming established, was to further an interaction of existing portraiture art with the daguerreotype. To meet expenses from costly experiments, Morse charged the general public for his daguerreotype portraits and besides this taught many pupils the photographic process for a fee.[5] He instilled in his students the basic rudiments of art he had learned from his many years of study—the precepts of lighting, proportions, and posing of the subject. Many Morse-inspired pupils became leading daguerreian artists of the period and a few brought honor and distinction, through exhibitions, to America and to their profession. Some of these famous names were Edward Anthony, Mathew Brady, Samuel Broadbent, F. A. Barnard, and Albert S. Southworth. Most students, after mastering the art, gave instruction to others, as well as taking portraits, thus following the tradition of many painters. Samuel Morse's techniques would serve as a guide to his followers.

A study of early daguerreotype portraiture reveals that paintings by the old masters were seriously studied by scholars of the new art medium. Also, daguerreian artists gathered ideas from various art sources including early American portraiture. Many daguerreotype portraits, especially those with natural outdoor or painted backgrounds, reflect old colonial portraits which had been inspired from British mezzotints. Mid-eighteenth-century portrait paintings, both American and European, were used as models for the daguerreian art. American primitive art coming in strongly at the close of the eighteenth century appears to have had a powerful effect on the new medium, particularly during the first few years of the art. Its influence may have been due, in part, to the fact that many limners and miniature portrait painters turned to daguerreotyping after the advent of the camera. The charming simplicity of American native art with little or no ornamentation is seen in many photographic examples done in the 1840 decade. The portrait, "Mrs. Freake and Baby Mary," dated 1674, typifies the colonial influence on the daguerreian's treatment of the mother and child theme. A painting by Ralph Earl, "William Carpenter," dated 1779, portrays a man seated on a chair, a hat on the table beside him and a book held in his hand. This was a familiar pose used by the daguerreian artist. English portraiture undoubtedly inspired the treatment of many female and child subjects. The painting by Sir Joshua Reynolds, "Lady Betty Hamilton," dated 1758, shows a girl holding flowers; many of Reynolds's portraits were certainly followed by students of the new art. A neoclassical influence was reflected in many daguerreotype portraits. The simple Grecian urn was introduced as an ornament; Roman pedestals and Grecian columns were sometimes used; the total effect of subject, object, lighting, all relating to the whole, gave a classical effect.

For the daguerreian artist, as with the painter, lighting was of prime importance. His best indoor work could be produced in a room with a large skylight. However, if a skylight arrangement was not available, his next choice was a room with a large window having a northwestern light aspect.[6] In the latter situation, the subject was placed between the direct rays of light coming in the window and those reflected back by the use of a white curtain and oftentimes a looking glass. Care had to be taken to place the white curtain opposite the window in such a manner that the light would reflect on the portion of the subject which was in the shade. Also, the reflected light had to be directed upward to accentuate the shaded side of the subject's countenance. A looking glass could be used effectively for this purpose. Sometimes diffused light was used in conjunction with dark-colored curtains for the skillful arrangement of shadings to blend the portrait.[7]

In addition to suitable lighting, a compatible background behind the sitter was important. In the early 1840's, outdoor nature often provided an artistic setting for the portrait. Also during the 1840's and later, engravings or a painting served as a backdrop.[8] A drapery swag to the side of the portrait gave the effect of a total painting. In the late 1840's, a new background technique was introduced for artistic representation. J. H. Whitehurst of Richmond, Virginia, used a background which was set in motion during the taking of the photograph. It was said to have produced a distinctness and boldness in the image and "gave the appearance of a beautifully clouded sky." [9] John A. Whipple, of Boston, Massachusetts, patented in 1849 a "revolving background" which gave the effect of a cloudy appearance very much like that usually given to portraits of faces done in crayon.[10] An opaque or partially opaque screen with an aperture was placed between the camera and the sitter. When the picture was being formed in the camera, the screen was moved slightly and gently up and down laterally in various directions so as to prevent any defined outline of the aperture of the screen from being formed on the picture. In this manner, a beautiful blending of the outline of the aperture with the background resulted and kept from the camera's eye any parts of the dress or person that were not desired. Mr. Whipple named these daguerreotypes "Crayon Portraiture." The most common of all background techniques used by daguerreians was a movable cloth-covered frame, which was usually six to twelve feet long and six to eight feet high, supported by posts at the ends. This frame was placed behind the sitter for the purpose of concentrating the rays of light which would give a desired tone to the surface on the finished daguerreotype plate. Another background frame developed by the profession consisted of two wooden frames, one on feet covered with light yellow canvas or cloth, sometimes perforated; it stood perpendicular to the floor, the lower part attached to another frame by means of hinges rising at an angle of forty-four degrees. This part of the frame was covered with a piece of black or brown lace dyed to the desired tint. This was called a "Chromatic Background." [11] Other background material used for the portrait would depend upon the whim of the individual artist.

In posing the patron, the daguerreian used his camera to give his subject a more attractive image. As painters many times removed scars, moles, and made long noses shorter, the daguerreian artist by raising and depressing his camera attained many flattering results. If a subject's forehead was broad, high, and intellectual, while the lower part of the face was thin, the camera was placed slightly lower than the chin and the head thrown a little forward.[12] If the head was small and the face full and heavy, the camera was elevated while the head and body were brought slightly forward. If a sitter was cross-eyed, his defect was overcome by directing the eye toward an object in the opposite quarter or else both eyes were turned toward an opposite object.[13] In the minute detail shown by the daguerreotype image, the freckled face posed a problem. A perfect complexion was achieved for portraiture by rubbing the face until very red.[14] Another method was to rub the face with a soft scarlet flannel cloth and to have the light fall directly on the cheek. This effected a lessening of contrast and with the photographic intensity being now nearly equal, a clear complexion could be produced. In overcoming a subject's defects, some of these portraits required a longer exposure than others, but this judgment rested on the part of the artist. It is possible, too, that daguerreians used make-up in the form of blackening about the eyes and parts of the face to add to the effect of an oil painting. There is some evidence that this was done.

It was said of Gilbert Stuart, American portrait painter, that he made it a point to keep his sitters talking so that a free and easy relationship might be established. The daguerreian artist by the mid-nineteenth century went to great lengths to put his sitters at ease not only during the actual taking of the portrait but before. Many notable daguerreians in America provided luxurious surroundings for their patrons. William A. Pratt, of Richmond, Virginia, advertised his reception room as "pretty as a boudoir, elegantly fitted up with splendid carpets, rich velvet divans, statuettes, immense bay window with stained glass."[15] Solomon N. Carvalho of Charleston, South Carolina, an artist of the brush as well as a daguerreian and a former member of Frémont's fifth expedition to the western frontier, publicized that his gallery was adorned with many specimens of paintings, engravings, and daguerreotypes.[16] Mathew Brady displayed in his New York gallery daguerreotype portraits of distinguished Americans and notable Europeans. A few galleries offered, besides art displays, nature exhibits of minerals, shells, stuffed birds, and other curiosities. The underlying theme used for atmosphere and advertising inducements was one of art and nature.

As the 1840 decade progressed, advertising became more elaborate. One established artist advertised in 1846, "Beautiful likenesses of Little Children, which I warrant to make satisfactory to parents/If they call upon me between the hours of 11 and 2, when the sky is clear." Mathew Brady advertised in 1852, "We have never seen anything finer than the tone of light in the room designed for taking children's pictures." Also advertised were the copying of oil paintings, miniatures, and sculpture. One famous daguerreian artist publicized in 1846, "We take great pains to have miniatures of deceased persons agreeable and satisfactory, and they are often so natural as to seem, even to Artists, in a quiet sleep."[17] This was not an isolated instance.[18] Photographing the dead had become an art in itself. In an age when death was a familiar figure, the last portrait of a loved one filled an emotional need. The daguerreian artist created an artistic and attractive death scene for his lasting portrait. Sometimes the coffin was used as a background; most often the artist photographed his subject reclining on a couch, one covered with printed material.[19] This relaxed pose gave the appearance of peaceful sleep. Flowers, usually roses or lilies, were laid across the chest of the departed. Lighting and drapery were important to the total effect. The daguerreian artist was also called upon to photograph monuments, burial plots, and to take lasting portraits of grieving mothers and widows.[20]

Artists of the brush, even those skeptical of the new art medium in the early years, came to rely on the camera's realistic eye for their portraits, especially for paintings of famous and busy people who had little time for innumerable sittings. Examples of combining the work of photographer and artist were displayed in the gallery of Mathew Brady. Brady had taken daguerreotypes of Daniel Webster, John C. Calhoun, and Henry Clay during 1849 and 1850. After the introduction of the wet-plate collodion process in the 1850's, he photographed these daguerreotypes on glassplate negatives. By use of magic lantern slides, the image was magnified to life size and transferred to canvas ready for painting. Brady then employed two prominent artists, John F. Neagle of Philadelphia and Henry F. Darby of Washington, to paint these life-sized portraits on canvas. The Webster portrait was done by Neagle; Clay and Calhoun by Darby. The paintings were on display for many years in Brady's Washington gallery. Later in the century they were purchased from Brady by the joint committee of the Library for Decoration of the Capitol and were displayed in the main corridor of the Senate.[21]

The increasing popularity and usefulness of the new art led to commercialism of the daguerreotype. Perhaps in the fierce competition of the early 1850's, the daguerreian lost some of his creativeness, although there are many exceptions. As the costuming of the 1850 decade became more elaborate and homes and hotels more ornate, the daguerreotype portrait became surrounded by too much embellishment. Also, other photographic methods, easier to produce, were making their way from England to America. The glass photograph, which would be named Ambrotype, became increasingly popular, and the paper photograph, already advanced in Europe, speeded the downfall of the American daguerreotype. In 1856, the tintype had its beginning and by 1860 the death of the daguerreotype was in sight.

In the twenty year period from 1840 to 1860, the daguerreian artist, using a camera for his drawing and chemicals for his paints, had created a powerful art. His drawings from the camera's eye in a brief period of history left for posterity a lasting portrait of an age.

1. PORTRAIT OF A LADY. Daguerreotype, c. 1845. LORENZO G. CHASE

2. COUNTRY COUPLE. Daguerreotype, c. 1844. ARTIST UNKNOWN

3. AMERICAN GOTHIC. Oil on Canvas, 1930. GRANT WOOD

4. PORTRAIT OF A MAN. Daguerreotype, c. 1844. ARTIST UNKNOWN

5. Sea Captain. Oil on Canvas, c. 1830. ARTIST UNKNOWN

Smithsonian Institution, Van Alstyne Collection

6. PROFILE. Daguerreotype, c. 1854. ARTIST UNKNOWN

7. SEATED GENTLEMAN. Daguerreotype, c. 1852. ARTIST UNKNOWN

8. LADY WITH FLOWERS. Daguerreotype, c. 1848. ARTIST UNKNOWN

9. Isaac Van Amburgh, Daguerreotype, c. 1850. artist unknown

10. Isaac Van Amburgh. Daguerreotype, c. 1850. artist unknown

11. Walt Whitman. Daguerreotype c. 1855. attributed to gabriel harrison

12. MAN WITH FRECKLES. Daguerreotype, c. 1841. ARTIST UNKNOWN

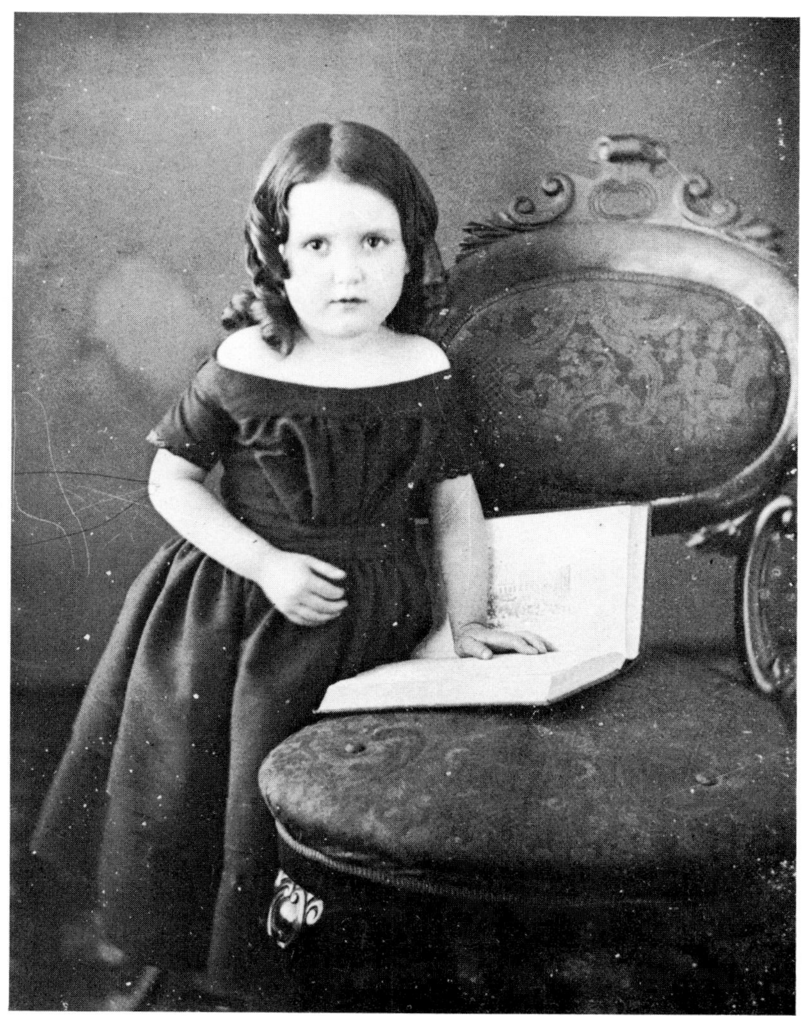

13. Child with Book. Daguerreotype, c. 1858. artist unknown

14. Boy with Hat. Daguerreotype, c. 1858. ARTIST UNKNOWN

15. Child with Sand Toy. Daguerreotype, c. 1859. artist unknown

16. Picking Wildflowers. Daguerreotype, c. 1848. S. HOYT

17. MAN WITH BABY. Daguerreotype, c. 1847. FULLER

18. MAN HOLDING DOG. Daguerreotype, c. 1853. ARTIST UNKNOWN

19. PORTRAIT OF AGED MAN. Daguerreotype, c. 1845. ARTIST UNKNOWN

20. Girl in Striped Dress. Daguerreotype, c. 1844. ARTIST UNKNOWN

21. Virginia Gentleman. Daguerreotype, c. 1850. FREDERICK LANGENHEIM

22. Young Man from Boston (probably henry d. thoreau). Daguerreotype, c. 1841. john plumbe, jr.

23. REVEREND F. F. D. MORGAN. Daguerreotype, c. 1850. ARTIST UNKNOWN

24. A Morgan of Hartford. Daguerreotype, c. 1843. MATHEW B. BRADY

25. CHILD ON DOG. Daguerreotype, c. 1850. ARTIST UNKNOWN

26. INDOOR SCENE. Daguerreotype, c. 1853. TUCKER

27. New England Sea Captain. Daguerreotype, c. 1843. L. C. CHAMPNEY

28. LADY IN BLUE. Daguerreotype, c. 1843. ARTIST UNKNOWN

29. Artist in Smock. Daguerreotype, c. 1853. artist unknown

30. Portrait by the Pedestal. Daguerreotype, c. 1848. nathaniel c. jaquith

31. THE TWO BAKERS. Daguerreotype, c. 1849. ARTIST UNKNOWN

32. SURVEYOR. Daguerreotype, c. 1854. ARTIST UNKNOWN

33. VIGIL BY THE COFFIN. Daguerreotype, c. 1848. ARTIST UNKNOWN

34. The Mourners. Daguerreotype, c. 1856. attributed to marcus root

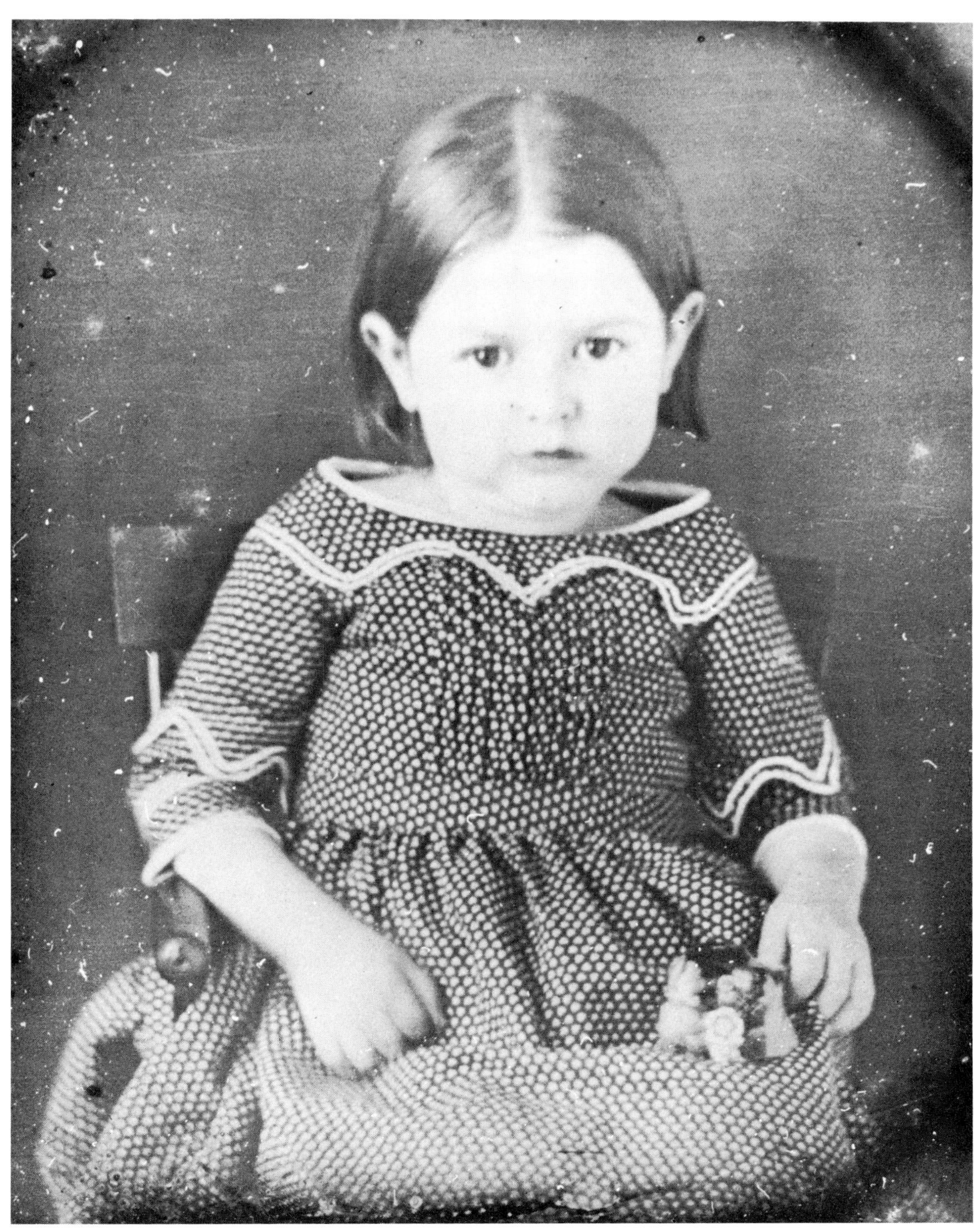

35. GIRL HOLDING FLOWERS. Daguerreotype, c. 1845. MATHEW B. BRADY

36. Two Boys. Daguerreotype, c. 1855. ARTIST UNKNOWN

37. LADY WITH SHAWL. Daguerreotype, c. 1842. ARTIST UNKNOWN

38. LADY IN BLACK. Daguerreotype, c. 1849. ARTIST UNKNOWN

39. SMILING BABY. Daguerreotype, c. 1854. ARTIST UNKNOWN

40. PORTRAIT OF A WOMAN. Daguerreotype, c. 1852. ARTIST UNKNOWN

41. Man in Straw Hat. Daguerreotype, c. 1855. artist unknown

42. Boy Orator. Daguerreotype, c. 1848. artist unknown

43. MATILDA GIBBS. Daguerreotype, c. 1858. ARTIST UNKNOWN

44. PORTRAIT OF A YOUNG LADY. Daguerreotype, c. 1848. ARTIST UNKNOWN

45. VIGNETTE. Daguerreotype, c. 1854. ARTIST UNKNOWN

46. Young Lady in Arbor. Daguerreotype, c. 1853. artist unknown

47. UNKNOWN OIL PAINTING. Daguerreotype, c. 1852. ARTIST UNKNOWN
Copy of Painting

48. Painting of Mr. and Mrs. William Walter Smith. Ambrotype Copy, c. 1856.
attributed to zedekiah belknap

2

Color Comes to the Portrait

The only ingredient lacking for an art daguerreotype to compete with a painter's rendition of portraiture was color. After overcoming mechanical and chemical difficulties of the new photographic process, the American daguerreian artist sought to emulate miniature portrait painters by hand coloring and gilding his silver plate. If a daguerreian did not have natural talent with the brush, he employed miniature painters or limners to do this exacting work. Fine native craftmanship and styling used in the creation of the new art medium combined with esthetic coloring produced portraiture of an appealing and magnetic quality.

An important and first step in introducing color to the daguerreotype was the toning of the reflected image. In the summer of 1840 a Frenchman named Fizeau recommended a solution using gold chloride; it was quickly and universally adopted.[1] This manipulation was called "gilding"; the total effect of the portrait was softened and it produced a warm tone and highlights. It also gave the surface of the daguerreotype plate great durability. On March 28, 1842, the first American patent was issued for coloring a daguerreotype to Benjamin R. Stevens and Lemuel Morse of Lowell, Massachusetts.[2] The method was a simple one. The finished daguerreotype was protected by a transparent solution of varnish or gum. Thus prepared, paints and colors could be applied to the surface of the portrait.

Seven months later, Daniel Davis of Boston patented a more complex process which was assigned to John Plumbe, Jr., of Boston, who was America's first nationally known promoter of photography.[3] The method was one of gilding the image on the daguerreotype plate by the use of a galvanic battery, using a positive wire immersed in one of three solutions: sulphate of copper, water, and cyanuret of potassium; gold dissolved in "aqua regia," then the adding of cyanuret of potassium; chloride of silver dissolved in cyanuret of potassium. The solution used, of course, was according to the tint desired with the basic metallic agent being copper, gold, or silver. If a deeper tint was wanted on the face rather than on the dress, a positive pole or wire of battery was held longer in the solution above the desired area. In using this method a uniform tint was obtained over the whole surface of the plate. The wire was actually used as a pencil, making deposits on the silvered plate with transparent color. The gilding of the plate in this manner improved the lights and shades of the portrait. This method was undoubtedly the one Plumbe referred to in his advertisement of 1843 in which he publicized, "Patent Colored Photographs." He stated: "The proprietor has lately discovered and patented an entirely new process by means of which he is now enabled to produce Colored Photographs, the superiority of which is so great as to defy all attempts at competition."[4] The price was three dollars. This method of "gilding" apparently did not last very long with most daguerreians as many pictures "so treated were clouded and spoiled."[5] The generally adopted method used by most artists was "gilding" with a gold solution by the agency of heat (a spirit lamp used on the rear of the plate to evaporate the solution) without the use of a galvanic arrangement. The variations of gilding methods and manipulations, both of timing and chemicals, must have been numerous, and a decision was therefore made by individual artists.

In may of 1843, a color patent was issued to Warren Thompson of Philadelphia which was assigned to Montgomery P. Simons, pioneer daguerreian artist of the same city. In this process, the finished daguerreotype portrait was steeped first in a gum solution; this was followed by the application, with a camel's hairbrush, of a grease of milky consistency to the parts of the plate not to be colored. The plate was then immersed in a solution which contained pure gold held in solution by cyanuret of potassium. A common electro-magnetic or galvanic battery was used, the negative pole of which was placed under the picture and the positive pole held over the portrait until the desired tint was acquired. After this process, the daguerreotype plate was washed off by steeping in boiling lye to remove the grease on the parts not colored.[6] If another tint was desired, the same process had to be followed using another metallic solution.

No other patents were issued for coloring until January 30, 1846. Frederick Langenheim, well-known daguerreian artist of Philadelphia, had bought a patent held by Isenring of Switzerland. However, Langenheim made an improvement on the original process in which he fixed his colors more permanently. Langenheim covered the parts of the completed portrait to be colored by using a powder of gum before the plate received color or during the process. The photographed daguerreotype plate in question was put in a frame, the edges of which projected up and even with the surface of the plate. It was fastened to the frame by pins. The parts of the picture to be colored were masked with a cutout stencil. The portrait was then placed in a box which had been previously shaken so that the heavier particles of the dry earth-color pigments used had partially settled. Timing was important. After the remaining fine color had settled on the portrait, sufficient heat was then applied to fuse the gum and color on the plate.[7]

The next color patent was forthcoming in the same year in March and was issued to William A. Pratt of Alexandria, Virginia. Pratt's process had a completely different idea than any to date. He finished his daguerreotype in the usual manner, including gilding. He then covered his silvered portrait with glass and proceeded to paint on the glass itself, using oil colors, any wanted design such as clouds, plain black walls, curtains, chairs, couches, and any desired accessories. The finished effect was similar to an oil painting. After the completion of his painting, he laid the daguerreotype onto the glass so that a complete junction of the two was formed from the adhesive nature of the varnish. It was then pressured until dry. His next step was to use nitric acid to reduce the thickness of the copper backing of the daguerreotype plate. After this was done any part of the picture could be cut away at the whim of the artist. A different picture, using the same process, could be attached to the first if desired. With this method, one or more portraits could be joined together. On completion, the picture presented an enameled appearance and the delicate image underneath was protected from air and dampness.[8] Actually, this was probably a first in trick photography. It is not known whether Pratt's process was used to any extent. It would seem doubtful because of its complex nature and amount of time required for preparation.

Despite the above color procedures, the great majority of daguerreian artists contented themselves with "gilding" their plates and protecting the finished picture with a thin coating of isinglass or other gum solution and completing the coloring by hand with dry pigment colors. Colors mostly used were carmine, Prussian blue, white, chrome yellow, yellow ochre, light red, indigo, burnt sienna, burnt umber, or mixed tints.[9] In Henry H. Snelling's book, *The History and Practice of the Art of Photography,* published in 1849, he urged his readers, "To study the coloring of the best artists, go to public galleries and view paintings, study the various styles of coloring, attitudes, folds of drapery and other points of art." He suggested a magnifying glass might be used to advantage. Coloring boxes were available to daguerreians. One type contained, "8 colors, a gold saucer, 4 sable pencils and a blender." The other box was more elaborate and contained "16 dry colors and tints; three for using wet; a bottle of gum water; an empty bottle for water; one gold and one silver saucer; 6 pencils and a blender."[10] After choosing his color, the artist rubbed it as fine as possible on a flat piece of glass (porphyry or agate) with another piece of the same material. The dry powder was then placed in a transparent goblet with water; it was well shaken to dilute the color and left to stand a few moments. When the thicker part had fallen to the bottom of the glass, the water on top was poured into another vessel. The remaining finer color particles deposited on the bottom of the glass were washed with anhydrous alcohol. After leaving the solution for some time, the alcohol was thrown away and the color collected and dried in the shade, keeping it away from dust. These colors were then ready to be placed on the daguerreotype portrait, immediately after completion, by means of a brush, making it adhere with a gentle rubbing.[11] On viewing poorly colored daguerreotypes, it is understandable why daguerreians often employed painters and limners.

The most startling and interesting development in the coming of color to the photograph was the bombshell announcement in *The Magic Buff,* a technical photography manual (November, 1850), by author and daguerreian Levi L. Hill, that a daguerreotype had been produced in color. Hill wrote, "Several years of experimentation have led us to the discovery of some remarkable facts in reference to the process of daguerreotyping in colors of nature. For instance, we can produce blue, red, violet and orange on one plate, at one and the same time."[12]

All over the country, newspapers eagerly publicized this great discovery—daguerreotype sales slumped. The anticipating, impatient public was waiting to have portraits captured in color!

Congratulations were in order after Mr. Hill's announcement, and efforts were made by the photographic industry to press Hill into making his process public. He patiently explained that while his process was complete, he was still having trouble producing yellows satisfactorily. He also wanted adequate compensation. (The U. S. Patent Office was unable to issue a patent to protect Hill's discovery.) [13]

By March 21, 1851, Hill had produced forty specimens of his daguerreotypes in color, three of which he described in detail: "A view, containing a red house, green grass and foliage, the wood color of trees, several cows of different shades of red and brindle, colored garments on the clothesline, blue sky and faint blue atmosphere intervening between the camera, and the distant mountains very delicately spread over the picture as if by the hand of a fairy artist";[14] the second one described was "a sunset scene, in which the play of colors on the clouds is impressed a truthfulness and gorgeous beauty which I cannot describe"; the third description related "Several portraits, in which I have the true complexion of the skin, the rosy cheeks and lips, blue and hazel eyes, auburn, brown and sandy hair, and every color of drapery." Hill also went on to say: "I have a most exquisite type of my little girl (one year old) [15] taken in the act of crying, the plate not having been exposed a full second. At the same time my light required 15 seconds for a daguerreotype. The picture has caught the expression perfectly, both of the eye and the whole face. On one cheek is seen a bright tear-drop, and the color showing through it much deeper than the surrounding parts; which latter, I suppose is owning to the refractive action of the fluid."[16]

As time went on Hill still did not reveal his process for "hillotypes" to the general public—"the invisible goblins of the yellows" were continuing to cause him trouble. However, many prominent artists and daguerreians visted Hill at his Catskill Mountains home.[17] John F. FitzGibbon, daguerreian of St. Louis, Missouri, visited Hill in the summer of 1852 and saw many color specimens. He later wrote in a published letter that he was "particularly impressed with one that had been taken from a highly colored lithograph on a double-whole sized plate of a lady and child . . . bright red, pink, dark blue, light blue and orange with their several combinations and tints." Another plate he described as "a basket of fruit, containing peaches, black and white grapes, with beautiful bright green and darkly tinted leaves."[18] Also, other hillotypes noted were "different varieties of flowers of the richest coloring and their tints."[19]

Additional hillotypes seen and described by other visitors and Hill included portraits of known living persons, various plates of colored prints, copies of paintings, a rosebush, a blackberry bush, Hill's daughter posed on a trunk,[20] a large color lithograph of the village of Prattsville, N. Y., and a laboring man with sunburned face, blue eyes, auburn hair, red-flannel shirt, and red and blue cravat.

Meanwhile, Hill had been denounced in various publications as being a fraud because of his refusal to make his invention public.[21] To refute these contentions, Hill sought the eyewitness testimony of America's leading inventor, Samuel F. B. Morse, who was also a pioneer daguerreian and capable portrait painter. Morse, a man of recognized integrity, visited Hill in September, 1852, viewed Hill's process, and was convinced. One of the hillotypes noted by Morse was that of a bird of plumage, taken in two seconds, which showed conclusively that the blues, yellows, and reds were distinctively given and fixed.[22] Morse's statement substantiated Hill's claim—". . . who builds must build on your foundadation."[23] In Europe, Becquerel and Niépce de St. Victor, working along similar lines, had produced photographs in color but had not been able to make the color permanent.[24]

Hill continued working on his discovery, despite personal difficulties, until about 1855 when he asked, through the medium of the press, the daguerreians who might still be interested to write him regarding his heliochromatic process. He also said he was still having trouble with the "yellows." When Hill finally published his book *A Treatise on Heliochromy* in 1856, the interest in color daguerreotypes was as dead as the method itself. Some daguerreians had worn black armbands back in 1854 to mark the passing of the daguerreotype.[25] A new fad had swept America—the ambrotype, a photograph on glass. As a matter of fact, when Hill's book was published, he was almost two fads behind popular fancy—the tintype had its beginning in the same year.

The making of a hillotype was explained in detail in Hill's book.[26] Chemical instructions were included in his formula. The plate to be prepared was first cleaned and then electrotyped in a chemical solution until it assumed a deep blue. Next, exposure to a series of separate chemicals and compounds resulted in the plate turning a bright pink color. From there, diffused light, heat, and more chemical reaction produced a light bluish cast to the plate. The plate was then placed in a jar of chlorine gas until it turned a faint yellow. If kept in total darkness, the plate would be ready when wanted for use. To render the plate sensitive, it was necessary to immerse it in a special solution until it appeared almost black (candlelight was suggested for this operation) and then, after being rinsed by water and dried, at that point it would reproduce colors by prolonged exposure to the image. The plate was then placed in a "quickner" solution to reduce the exposure time necessary. To increase the strength and brilliancy of the picture, the plate could be heated until it assumed a red or it could be exposed to the action of orange rays of light. After the plate was placed in a camera and exposed, a developer was used to bring out the latent color images. The plate was then fixed and finished by first immersing in a solution, then rinsing and drying. A polish was applied with a soft buckskin if desired.

Morse said in referring to Hill's process: "It must be in the hands of no ordinary man, but will require the production of the perfect picture, the taste, the skill, the feeling of thorough and accomplished artists."[27]

Hill frankly said he could not chemically explain why he produced color photographs. The only explanation he made in reference to the preparation of plates was "On this one thing, molecular arrangement—the whole phenomenon of coloration depends."

Levi Hill, after nine long years of experimenting with dangerous chemicals and fumes, and after failing to receive recognition or honor for his labors in the photography world, left the field of daguerreian art in 1856. He had mixed the chemicals for his "sun paintings" (as he liked to call them) with the same care that the old masters mixed their paints.

An interesting daguerreotype picture-taking technique was patented by Henry E. Insley of New York on January 6, 1852. Insley's process had to do with bringing out or casting a halo of various tints around the image. His daguerreotype plate was prepared in the usual manner, except that he used a light or white background. His method was involved with the mercury bath which was the last step before "fixing" the portrait. The daguerreotype plate with the latent image was placed in a closed box which was heated to 167 degrees Fahrenheit. The mercury vapor developed the image. Insley placed on the frame of his mercury bath a mat of an oval, square, or another desired form, which had an opening of about one third or one half the size of the daguerreotype plate to be used. On top of the mat was placed a small frame which raised the daguerreotype plate about three sixteenths of an inch from the mat. The frame was made so that the mercury fumes could pass freely upon the center of the daguerreotype plate and would gradually diminish toward the outer edges producing varied tints and giving strength and relief to the image. Insley claimed the tints were more beautiful after the plate was gilded in the final step of the procedure. He also said that "Daguerreotypists from almost every part of the country have seen them and pronounce them the prettiest portraits that have yet been got up."[28] He named them "Illuminated Daguerreotypes" and was awarded a silver medal for these by the American Institute.

An item in *Humphrey's Journal* during the same year carried an idea for tinting a daguerreotype. A substitution for mercury, a protoiodide of the same metal was used successfully. "This compound is of a fine green, and is obtained by pounding together in equal quantities iodine and mercury, moistened with a few drops of alcohol. It is to be washed as usual—first covering the iodide with a fine muslin."[29]

It is certain that many of the daguerreian artists were also master chemists. Some of the daguerreotype backgrounds as seen on plate examples are ivory white, some have a greenish tinge, others have a deep brown or golden color. Secrecy, because of intense competition, shrouded many improvements especially those of a chemical nature such as mercury bath and gilding.

If a daguerreian artist lacked the simplicity so charming in the 1840 decade, he compensated in the 1850's with his successful, pleasing, and sometimes startling specimens of the daguerreian art in color.

49. Eugenie Bayley. Daguerreotype, c. 1851. levi l. hill

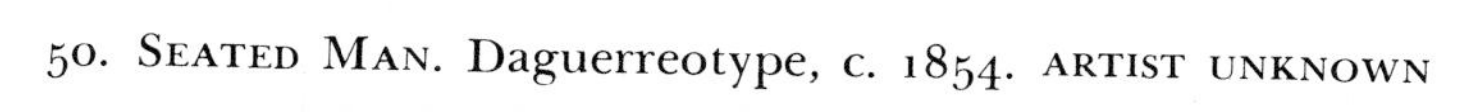

50. Seated Man. Daguerreotype, c. 1854. artist unknown

51. LADY IN A RIDING HABIT. Oil on Canvas, 1856. GUSTAVE COURBET
Metropolitan Museum of Art, Bequest of Mrs. H. O. Havemeyer, 1929, the H. O. Havemeyer Collection

52. Lady in a Riding Habit. Daguerreotype, c. 1856. artist unknown

53. Mary Hill. Daguerreotype, 1852. LEVI L. HILL

54. Brandy Legs. Ambrotype, c. 1858. ARTIST UNKNOWN

55. Country Boy. Daguerreotype, c. 1852. LEVI L. HILL

57. Unknown Painting. Daguerreotype, c. 1858.
RUFUS ANSON

56. Man with Red Beard. Talbotype,
c. 1850. FREDERICK LANGENHEIM
See Plate 21 for Comparison

58. LADY WITH FURS. Daguerreotype, c. 1855. ARTIST UNKNOWN

59. THE GOLDEN PORTRAIT. Daguerreotype,
c. 1847. LORENZO G. CHASE

60. Lady in Red. Daguerreotype, c. 1849. john hewitt

3

The Daguerreian Scene

AMERICA'S POETIC ARTIST, GEORGE FULLER, WROTE HIS FATHER FROM BOSTON ON APRIL 11, 1840: "You have heard much of the daguerreotype, or drawings produced by rays of light upon a plate chemically prepared. Augustus and I went to see the specimens, and were much pleased; our ticket would entitle us to one of the lectures, but we were too late, as they had ceased delivering them." Fuller was referring to the Boston lectures of Francois Gouraud, Daguerre's pupil who was sent to America to establish an agency for the sale of cameras and apparatus and to demonstrate Daguerre's process. George Fuller did buy a camera and equipment and brought it back to the family farm at Deerfield in the Connecticut Valley, where he took a daguerreian scene of the old homestead.[1] The incident of George Fuller shows the curiosity and interest with which artists regarded the new art medium of photography. Whether Fuller ever made use of the camera as a tool for preliminary drawings for his paintings is not known, but many artists did find the "Instantaneous View" an invaluable aid to their brush.

John Mix Stanley, celebrated painter of Indians, was one of the artists who explored the dual use of the camera and the brush. Stanley had become established in Detroit in 1834 as a portrait painter. Interested in the frontier, he made several excursions into the wilderness at various times from 1838–1848; he traveled to New Mexico, California, Oregon, and the Columbia River. After the advent of the camera, Stanley became active as a daguerreian artist in Washington, D. C., during 1842.[2] In the spring of 1853, following a tradition of artists, he accompanied a survey of a northern railroad route to the Pacific, under the command of I. I. Stevens. Stanley's activity with his camera is mentioned by Stevens: "Mr. Stanley commenced taking daguerreotypes of the Indians with his apparatus. They are delighted and astonished to see their likenesses produced by the direct action of the sun. They worship the sun, and they consider Mr. Stanley was inspired by their divinity and he thus became in their eyes a great medicine man."[3] Stanley's excellent portrayal of the racial characteristics of Indians was undoubtedly influenced by his realistic camera images. Also, his profound landscapes of mountain slopes and water possibly stem from some of his daguerreian art scenes. Unfortunately, Stanley's daguerreotypes probably perished in the Smithsonian fire which destroyed most of his Indian paintings.

As artists swarmed about the countryside in this era, so too did the daguerreians take to the open road in search of patrons. They fitted up wagons with cameras and equipment and were ready to take both scene or portrait on little notice. Some ingenious daguerreians floated along the Mississippi River with well stocked flatboat galleries. Sometimes, the man with the camera, as the man with the brush, settled in a rural town for a month or two and then moved on. If a moment in history was to be recorded, a daguerreian was assigned to take the view. For example, see plate 70 of the Town Hall, Lebanon, New Hampshire. When the Town Hall was moved from its original site in 1851, a view was taken. A painting of the same scene, possibly based on the daguerreotype, hangs in the public library of Lebanon.[4]

Niagara Falls, one of nature's grandeurs and always a challenge to the painter, proved an intriguing subject for daguerreians. Daguerreotypes of the falls by J. H. Whitehurst, of Baltimore, Maryland, were exhibited in the Great Exhibition at the Crystal Palace in London, 1851. The scenes were described in glowing terms: "The cloud of spray rising from the bottom, and the white sheets of foam on the waters, contrasted with the trees and land, always exhibit a remarkable and interesting appearance in a daguerreotype. . . . The water of the falls in question appears as a white cloud."[5]

The panorama, popular from the 1830's, which depicted scenes painted on canvas in sections, and was accompanied by a lecture, probably led to the idea of photographing panoramic views, using several large-sized daguerreotype plates placed side by side to form a wide range picture. Charles Fontayne and William S. Porter in 1848, using eight large-sized daguerreotype plates, captured a magnificent scene encompassing a two mile view of the Ohio River from the town of Fulton to the end of Vine Street, Cincinnati. The delineation of detail on this panorama was so exact that even river boats could be identified. Another superb panoramic view was taken by William Shew, in 1852, of San Francisco from Rincon Point, using five plates. Fortunately, both these views are still in existence. Another influence stemming undoubtedly from the early panorama was the use of daguerreotype scenes for lecturing materials. Because of the small size of the daguerreotype, it was necessary to enlarge the scenic views that were to be illustrated by making oil paintings or pencil sketches from the original daguerreotypes. A California artist, J. Wesley Jones, claimed to have taken several hundred daguerreotypes of California—gold mines, the plains, and the Rocky Mountains. Jones lectured in the Eastern cities to attentive audiences, using pencil sketches and oil paintings copied from his daguerreotypes. He lectured in New York City, from 1853 to 1854, and advertised as, "Jones Pantoscope of California." [6]

Daguerreian artists were also commissioned to do pictorial work for publications. *Putnam's Monthly Magazine*, February, 1853, began a series of articles on cities; the first was titled, "New York Daguerreotyped." It was intended to show the progress of the city of New York, its architecture, hotels and restaurants, churches, colleges and schools, benevolent institutions, places of amusement, and even private dwellings. The pictures illustrating the articles were engravings copied from original daguerreotypes, which had been photographed expressly for this purpose.[7] Magazines and newspapers were unable to reproduce photographs in this era and had to rely heavily on engravers.

It is not known how strongly the realistic daguerreian scene influenced the Hudson River School or Romantic genre painting; however, the two did run parallel with the daguerreotype during this period. The Hudson River School, which stressed realism, came in strongly after 1840. Painters must have given thought to the possibilities of the new photographic process. Asher B. Durand, leading landscape artist of the era, remarked to Levi L. Hill, a daguerreian artist visting him: "Reproduce by the means of light, the beautiful colored image you see on the ground glass of your camera and you will be ahead of all painters."[8] Durand, as a former engraver, would have been quick to note the influence of the daguerreotype, which had an exacting minuteness of detail reflected on its silvered plate.

Samuel Morse's advice to painters, in 1840, to make use of the camera as a tool for landscape views must have been heeded by many. There is much evidence in existence of not only paintings based on the "instantaneous view," but a multitude of sketches, drawings, and lithographs, many of these made for illustrating. After the artist or engraver copied from the daguerreotype, the silver image was apparently then disregarded, having served its purpose, which would account for the great loss of early daguerreian scenes. However, the work of these pioneer daguerreian artists lives on, in a sense, in many existing art works which came into being in an important period of native American art.

61. The Lackawanna Valley. Oil on Canvas, 1855. GEORGE INNESS

National Gallery of Art, Washington, D.C., Gift of Mrs. Huttleston Rogers

62. Valley of Clouds. Ambrotype, c. 1858. artist unknown

63. NIAGARA FALLS. Unfinished Oil on Photograph, c. 1856. FREDERICK CHURCH
Courtesy of The Cooper Union Museum

64. NIAGARA FALLS. Daguerreotype, c. 1855. ARTIST UNKNOWN

Collection of Miss Josephine Cobb

65. COUNTRY FAIR. Ambrotype, c. 1856. ARTIST UNKNOWN

ERRATA

TABLE OF CONTENTS:

For Acknowledgments, page vii
read Acknowledgments, page iv;
for List of Illustrations, page xi
read List of Illustrations, page vii

LIST OF ILLUSTRATIONS:

There should be no listing for Frontispiece
which is not included in book

Page 76: Plate 63 is printed upside down

66. A DAY AT THE MILL. Daguerreotype, c. 1850. ARTIST UNKNOWN

67. Rural Home. Daguerreotype, c. 1850. artist unknown

68. The Welcome. Daguerreotype, c. 1842. artist unknown

69. Gold Mining Camp, Jamestown, California. Daguerreotype, c. 1851. ARTIST UNKNOWN

70. LEBANON, NEW HAMPSHIRE. Daguerreotype, c. 1851. ARTIST UNKNOWN

71. A Village Ceremony. Ambrotype, c. 1857. ARTIST UNKNOWN

72. New England Factory Village. Ambrotype, c. 1856. mc intosh and sterlin

4

Miniature Cases for Daguerreian Art

THE FIRST PUBLIC MENTION IN AMERICA OF A CASE WHICH CONTAINED A DAGUERREOTYPE was a New York newspaper account in the *Morning Herald,* September 30, 1839. The account described a daguerreotype scene of part of St. Paul's Church which was made by a Mr. Seager, an Englishman residing in the city. The article went on to say: "It is the first time that the rays of the sun were ever caught in this continent, and imprisoned in all their glory and beauty, in a morocco case, with golden clasps." The same report said the image was on a small piece of copper equal in size to a miniature painting. This last statement is an important clue as very little is known as to the origin of the daguerreotype case.

Toward the end of the eighteenth century, a rectangular case was often used to contain a miniature portrait painting rather than the usual oval one; miniatures had also become larger. The rectangular miniature painting was boxed in a shallow leather covered case with a plush lining, and it became a small picture to stand on a desk.[1] Miniature painters were actively engaged in producing likenesses of Americans when "sun paintings," as the daguerreian art was often called, became available to the general public. It is reasonable to assume that existing cases which held miniature paintings would be used by pioneers of the new photographic art medium for their silvered images. Probably jewel cases were also used if they were of the right size to hold a standard sized daguerreotype. Mathew Brady, a jewel casemaker in 1843, before he actively became a daguerreian artist, often provided cases to daguerreians.[2]

The most common type of daguerreotype case was made of wood; it had a shallow top and bottom piece which was hinged together with the same paper-thin leather as its covering. The inside of the right or bottom piece was edged around its perimeter with a narrow strip of velvet plush; placed inside this opening was the picture, which was protected further by a gold-colored mat, overlaid with a piece of glass. Sometimes, around the then sealed picture, was placed a "protector," a thin brass frame; its edges pressed down firmly around the whole, giving a neat framed appearance as well as added protection. The side of the case opposite the portrait was padded with silk, satin, or velvet in shades of purple, red, green, or blue. The case when closed was fastened with one or two hooks. The standard American daguerreotype plates came in six sizes, ranging from "six and one half by eight and one half inches," to a small size of "one and three quarters by one and five eighths inches." The most popular size by far was the "sixth" size, which measured "two and three quarters by three and one quarter inches." Daguerreotype cases were made to fit these specifications. Only the Americans and the English were distinctive in the use of cases for preserving their daguerreotypes. The Europeans framed theirs with a cutout matting under glass. The French called these "Passe-partout."

The making of miniature cases, especially for daguerreotypes, in the early days of photography is obscure, but it is likely that the cost factor was an influence on its beginnings, as moroccan cases of the type used for miniature paintings were expensive. Some of the earliest known daguerreotype cases have been examined and are found to have been constructed of wood, rather crudely handmade; their paper-thin leather coverings are lightly embossed with an overall small design.[3] The makers generally remain anonymous. However, a few early casemakers are known and examples of their cases show they carried simple embossed designs on their covers. Two of these early case embossings are both of classic design, the "Lyre" and "Grecian Urn with Flowers." Material for the coverings of these early wooden cases was taken from the outer half of split sheepskin, the kind that was used for bookbinding; moroccan or goatskin leather was also used for some case models but was expensive.[4] Embossings on the leather covers were produced by brass die cylinders which had raised figures and engraved designs; these were used in conjunction with a heavy screw press. In the 1840's, the decade when the leather-embossed cases reached their height, one of the only signed names to appear on any of the covers as a designer was that of "Pretlove." This would be David Pretlove, listed from 1844–1856 in New York City directories as an engraver, diesinker, and maker of cylinders for embossing. There is much evidence that casemakers "borrowed" each other's designs; one, so noted, was the "Delicate Rose" motif, which was the most preferred by daguerreians in the 1840's; it came in many varieties with the same general rose pattern.[5] Beginning about 1844, decorations on leather-covered cases became more varied and, by 1848, a very large assortment was offered.

Many daguerreotype stock companies bought their cases from a number of small makers, many from the New England area, to supply the growing number of daguerreians. One large manufacturer of daguerreian materials—Scovill Manufacturing Company, Waterbury, Connecticut—many times embossed its own designs on leather for the final step in finishing daguerreotype cases.[6] Brass dies for this purpose were often made by the company's own engraver, Hiram W. Hayden of Waterbury.[7] In the early 1850's, Edward Anthony, a large New York dealer in daguerreotype materials and former pioneer daguerreian artist, had four separate departments for the manufacture of daguerreotype cases. One department made the wooden boxes; another covered with leather and trimmed; one embossed the leather and added cushions, and a fourth department gilded the cases.[8] In 1854, the firm devised a press which would affix the leather or other covering material to the cases; prior to this, the embossed covers were glued to the wood surface and smoothed by the use of a spatula which often injured the appearance of the embossed figure.[9] With Anthony's new press, the design remained in sharp relief. The company also devised an easier method of inserting the silk-covered padding, again eliminating much handwork.[10]

An important adjunct to the Edward Anthony firm's business was the supplying of mats and preservers for daguerreotype cases. These were made from sheet brass by a powerful press driven by steam. There was a difference in cost for these depending upon the value of the metal used and the style of finishing. Three styles of mat shapes were available: the "oval," "fancy nonpareil," and "double elliptic." After the shapes were stamped into their respective designs, they were dipped into strong acids so that the surface of each assumed a "frosted" or "marked" appearance. They were then lacquered and steam dried.[11] The only difference in making a preserver was that the finish remained bright.

About 1850, some daguerreotype cases were produced in the shape of a book. Many of this type were fashioned of papier-mâché, inland with mother-of-pearl; others were covered with velvet, lined in watered silk (some of the latter cases were called "Jenny Lind," after the famous Swedish opera star, so admired in this period). Tortoise shell was also used to form cases which were sometimes inlaid with pearl and silver. Other book-style cases were covered with leather and etched with gold. The parts of these book-types cases, which resembled pages, were painted with gilt. Hinged fasteners clasped the lids on these cases to a closed position. Snap type closures were used on some models.

The material used in the manufacturing of the papier-mâché case was prepared by pasting or gluing sheets of paper together and submitting them to powerful pressure, so that the composition acquired a hardness of a board when dried. The pearls for the inlaid work were prepared in thin layers and cut with scissors or knives; some were of regular forms already stamped by a press. Each piece of pearl used to form a design was stuck upon a soft ground of japan varnish with which the case was finished. It was then hardened in a stove, varnished again, and again hardened. The black varnish was then rubbed off the pearl design with pumice stone and water. The "Aurora" pearl was preferred by designers because of its brilliant colors. Another method was to place pieces of white pearl of various thicknesses on the soft ground of varnish; powdered colors were then applied to the pearls as desired, and the whole was finished with colors mixed with vanish.[12] Many mother-of-pearl designs were also embellished with gold or silver work in the form of leaves and stems or scrolls. The richly colored ornamentation against a jet black background suggests a Chinese influence. In addition, some variations of book-type cases were decorated with hand-painted nature scenes on their covers with the outer edges inlaid with mother-of-pearl. The use of inlaid pearl work on these cases probably stemmed from the artistic snuffboxes which were popular throughout the eighteenth century. The snuffbox had been an esthetic creation of the jeweler, artist, and enameler of the earlier period.

A very interesting daguerreotype case was patented on March 8, 1853 by John F. Mascher of Philadelphia. His case was made for the usual standard size of daguerreotype plate and was converted into a stereoscope by a simple arrangement of a supplementary lid or flap, inside, into which were fitted two ordinary magnifying lenses. Mascher placed two stereoscopic images, in combined size to that of a standard size daguerreotype, opposite the hinged flap, so that when the flap was placed in an upright position after the case was opened, the viewer had an illusion of a three dimensional image by looking through the magnifying lens.[13] The invention was clever, portable, and compact; it offered the daguerreian patron a fascinating view in depth of himself. In 1855, Mascher patented a similar item, a stereoscopic medallion, which looked like an ordinary locket. This sold for twelve dollars.[14]

During the 1840's, photographing the dead became an important part of daguerreian art. Daguerreotype casemakers then presented designs which were suitable to contain the images of deceased persons. The Scovill Manufacturing Company carried a daguerreotype case for this purpose in about December, 1852. It was defined as a creation for "Likenesses of deceased persons, and for all sepulchral daguerreotypes—for which purpose they are peculiarly adopted. The designs are unique, the whole appropriate—rich without being gaudy."[15]

A radically new and different case appeared on the market in about 1853. However, leather-type cases still stayed popular throughout the 1850's. The new cases would become known as "Union Cases." In May, 1852, Samuel Peck, of New Haven, Connecticut, daguerreotypist and casemaker, began experimenting with making cases of plastic material. His idea probably originated from working with papier-mâché cases in which paper and heat were used. The basic ingredients for Peck's plastic material were sawdust ground as fine as flour, shellac, plus color, all of which, when heated and rolled, became plastic; the whole was then pressed into dies to make the completed design for the case. A heavy screw press machine was used to make pressure. Peck ran into some difficulty because his machinery couldn't stand the heats required for the process.[16] Then, too, the dies were larger than ordinarily used. Despite difficulties, a patent was issued to Peck on October 3, 1854 for the first thermoplastic daguerreotype case. In the patent, he describes materials used and tells of holding gilded paper directly against the surface of the die, compressing it upon the plastic composition.[17] The procedure not only gave a burnished impression to the case, but also strengthened it and was helpful in preventing cracking of the case when in use. A conventional arrangement of metal hinges was employed in the new case. A series of improvements on these hinges would be the basis for additional patent issues for other plastic cases in the years to come.

The images seen in bold relief on the covers of these plastic "Union Cases" are very impressive and reflect the art of the daguerreian era. The underlying themes for their molded designs were nature, history, religion, and patriotism. Also, many classical conventional motifs were used, their origins derived from ancient art sources. Some of the nature designs produced are of beautiful simplicity; for example, a scallop shell, its rounded curves effective against a plain background. Other more complex nature designs depicted baskets of flowers and various fruit motifs. Of the elaborate historical scenes represented, many were copied from famous paintings. Other skillfully etched scenes were inspired from lithographs or mezzotints. Expert engravers, who were also diesinkers, were commissioned to create the large variety of designs needed for the several competing plastic casemakers who flourished during the mid-1850's. Many of these attractive cases are signed on the cover by the designer; others, like "Country Life," see plate 80, elaborate in conception, remain unsigned. The thermoplastic case is highly prized by today's decorative arts collector.

It should be mentioned that in addition to paper-leather, papier-mâché and plastic cases, less impressive cases also were made during the 1850's, especially after the cheaper methods of photography (glass and paper) became popular. The coverings for these were made of embossed cloth, treated to be water repellent; also, some were of wood or just plain cardboard. Lockets and brooches were in existence to hold small daguerreotypes.

Daguerreotype cases, a by-product of daguerreian art, are interesting. They reflect the changing taste of the American public. The nature and classical theme, emphasized in the 1840 period, gradually gave way during the 1850's to more ornate designs and embellishment, which expressed the trend of the times. Among case designs, each group reflected its own distinct art.

73. The Calmady Children. Oil on Canvas, c. 1824. sir thomas lawrence
Metropolitan Museum of Art, Bequest of Collis P. Huntington, 1925

74. THE CALMADY CHILDREN. From the Original Painting by Sir Thomas Lawrence. Thermoplastic Daguerreotype Case, c. 1854–1857. CASEMAKER UNKNOWN; DESIGNER: HIRAM W. HAYDEN

75. The Grecian Urn. Embossed-Leather Daguerreotype Case, c. 1841–1846. casemaker: john plumbe, jr.

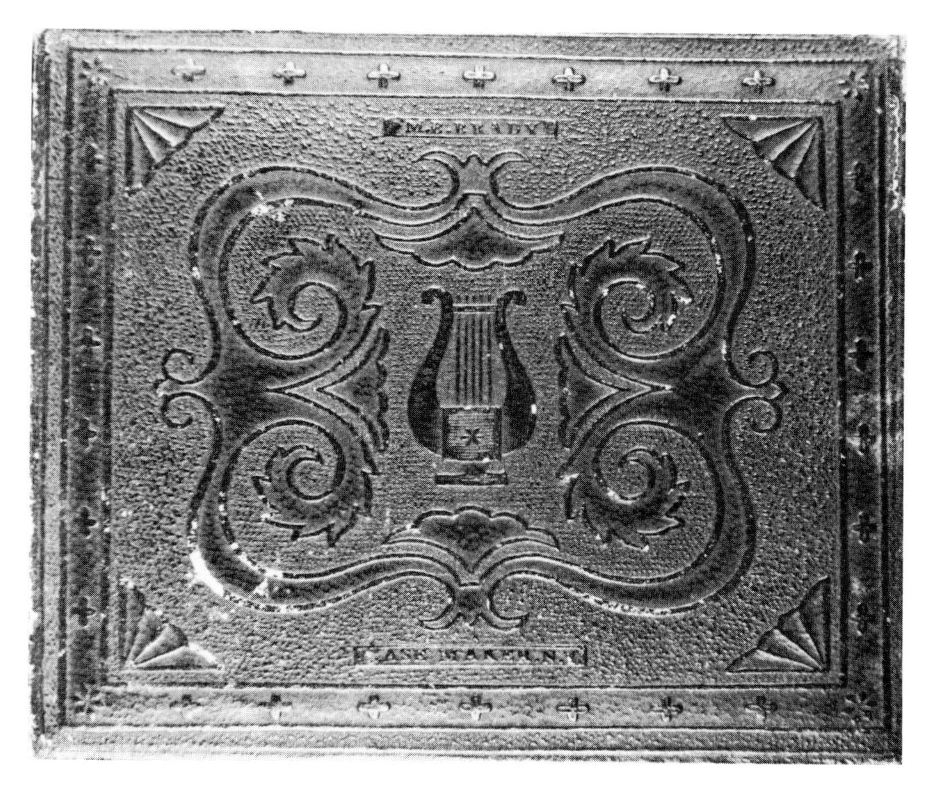

76. THE LYRE. Embossed-Leather Daguerreotype Case, c. 1842–1844.
CASEMAKER: M. B. BRADY

77. THE DELICATE ROSE. Embossed-Leather Daguerreotype Case, c. 1844–1849. CASEMAKER UNKNOWN

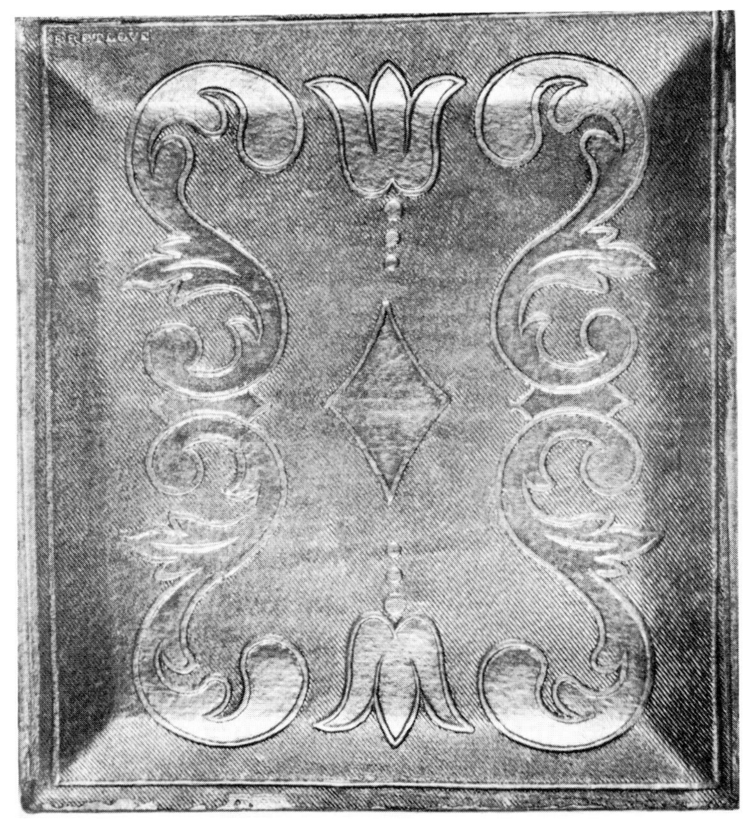

78. The Tulip. Embossed-Leather Daguerreotype Case, c. 1846–1850. DESIGNER: PRETLOVE

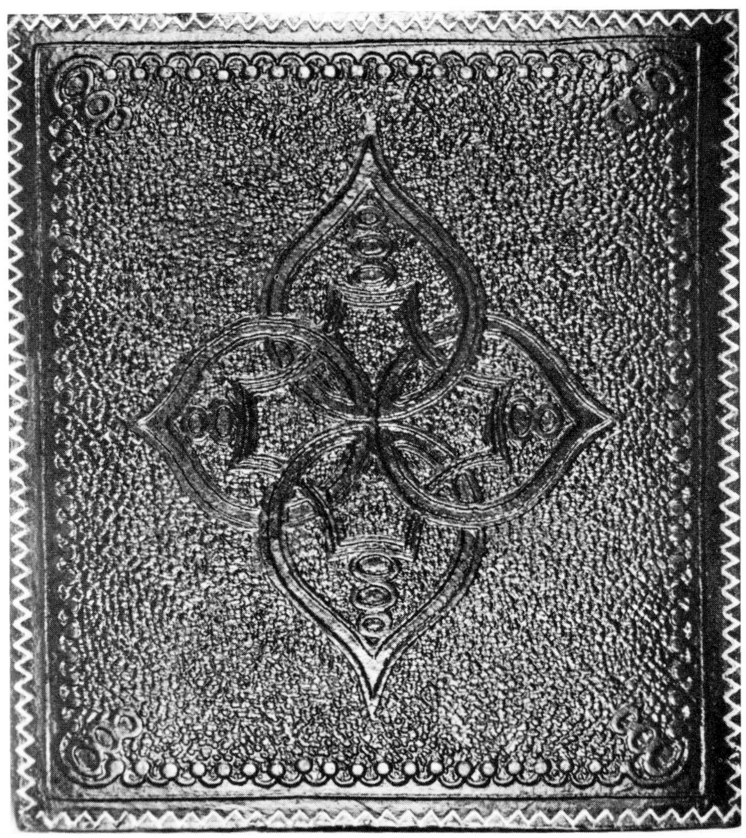

79. Oriental Motif. Embossed-Leather Daguerreotype Case, c. 1850–1855. CASEMAKER UNKNOWN

80. Country Life. Thermoplastic Daguerreotype Case, c. 1857. casemaker: critchlow; designer unknown

81. AMERICAN FARM. Thermoplastic Daguerreotype Case, c. 1858–1861. CASEMAKER: LITTLEFIELD, PARSONS, CO.; DESIGNER UNKNOWN

82. THE ROSE AND THE THISTLE. Thermoplastic Daguerreotype Case, c. 1858. CASEMAKER: SAMUEL PECK; DESIGNER: KEY

83. THE LAUNCHING. Thermoplastic Daguerreotype Case, c. 1853–1856. CASEMAKER UNKNOWN (Probably Manufactured by F. Goll) ; DESIGNER: GOLL

84. CUPID AND THE WOUNDED STAG. Thermoplastic Daguerreotype Case, c. 1857.
CASEMAKER: CRITCHLOW; DESIGNER UNKNOWN

85. The Chess Players. Thermoplastic Daguerreotype Case, c. 1856–1860. casemaker unknown; designer unknown

86. THE ANGEL HOLDING BABIES. Thermoplastic Daguerreotype Case, c. 1855–1856. CASEMAKER: SAMUEL PECK; DESIGNER UNKNOWN

87. Mountain Scene. Book-Type Daguerreotype Case with Hand Painted Scene, c. 1852–1858. artist unknown; casemaker unknown

88. Rose Motif. Book-Type Daguerreotype Case with Mother-of-Pearl Inlay, c. 1850–1858. ARTIST UNKNOWN; CASEMAKER UNKNOWN

89. SPRAY OF FLOWERS. Book-Type Daguerreotype Case with Mother-of-Pearl Inlay, c. 1850–1858. ARTIST UNKNOWN; CASEMAKER UNKNOWN

Notes to the Text

CHAPTER 1

1. M. A. Root, *The Camera and the Pencil* (New York: 1864), p. 360.

2. *U. S. Letters Patent,* 1,582 (May 8, 1840).

3. Henry Hunt Snelling, *The History and Practice of the Art of Photography* (New York: G. P. Putnam's, 1849), p. 57; Benjamin S. Silliman, Jr., *The American Journal of Science and Arts,* XL (April, 1841), 139.

4. A letter to Morse from E. N. Hordford, Albany, dated November 18, 1840, says: "I learn with equal astonishment and gratification, that you have succeeded in taking likenesses in ten seconds with diffused light." In Samuel Irenaeus Prime, *The Life of Samuel F. B. Morse* (New York: D. Appleton and Co., 1875), pp. 408, 409. Robert Taft in *Photography and the American Scene* (New York: The Macmillan Company, 1938), reprinted 1942, p. 44, states that accelerators (called "quicks") were in common use by 1841 and exposure was cut from minutes to seconds.

5. Robert Taft, pp. 37, 38. Taft states Morse's fee for instruction was "Twenty Five or Fifty dollars."

6. *Humphrey's Journal* (1852), p. 173.

7. Henry Hunt Snelling (1849), p. 40.

8. *Ibid.,* p. 41.

9. *Ibid.*

10. S. D. Humphrey, *American Handbook of the Daguerreotype* (New York: 1853), p. 131.

11. Henry Hunt Snelling, *A Dictionary of the Photographic Art* (New York: 1854), p. 12.

12. M. A. Root, p. 121.

13. *Ibid.*

14. *Ibid.*

15. *City Directory* (Richmond, Va.: Montague, 1852). Listed under advertisement number 12.

16. *City Directory* (Charleston, S. C.: Baget, 1852). Full-page advertisement.

17. *City Directory* (Boston: 1846). Advertisement for Southworth and Hawes establishment at 5½ Tremont Row.

18. *American Advertiser,* Prall, Lewis and Co. (New York: 1850). Many of the daguerreian's advertisements offered services for taking pictures of the deceased.

19. Daguerreotypes of the deceased exist in the authors' collection. Included are subjects with the body posed on couches with flowers on bosom or held in hands. Other such daguerreotypes are found in other collections.

20. *Humphrey's Journal,* IV (1852), p. 269.

21. Charles Fairman, *Art and Artists of the Capitol of the United States of America* (Washington, D. C.: U. S. Government Printing Office, 1927), pp. 294, 321.

CHAPTER 2

1. Robert Taft, p. 43.

2. *U. S. Letters Patent,* 2,522.

3. *U. S. Letters Patent,* 2,826.

4. *Albany Directory* (Albany, N. Y.: 1843). Full-page advertisement.

5. *U. S. Letters Patent,* 9,354 (October 26, 1852). In his patent Charles L'Homdieu of Charleston, S. C., states that earlier methods of gilding were abandoned by many daguerreians "for reason that a large portion of the pictures so treated were clouded and spoiled."

6. *U. S. Letters Patent,* 3,085 (May 12, 1843).

7. *U. S. Letters Patent,* 4,370 (January 30, 1846).

8. *U. S. Letters Patent,* 4,423 (March 14, 1846).

9. Henry H. Snelling (1849), p. 129.

10. *Ibid.,* p. 64.

11. *Humphrey's Journal,* V, 4, p. 88.

12. *The Magic Buff,* Levi L. Hill, IV, 1850.

13. In February, 1853, Hill wrote a petition to the U. S. Senate: ". . . my process, being strictly chemical in its nature could not find security in an ordinary Patent, I therefore appeal to your honorable body for some special provision as your wisdom may suggest . . . I ask, at least such an examination of my claim to this important discovery, as will tend to secure my native land the credit of the invention." (32 Congress, 2nd Session, No. 214.) On February 24, 1853, Hill's petition was referred to the Committee on Patents and the Patent Office. The answer was forthcoming on March 3, 1853 as follows:

32d Congress, 2d Session.	[SENATE.]	Rep. Com. No. 427.

IN SENATE OF THE UNITED STATES.

MARCH 3, 1853.—Ordered to be printed.

MR. JAMES made the following

REPORT.

The Committee on Patents and the Patent Office, to whom was referred the memorial of Levi L. Hill, in reference to his alleged discovery in heliochrome, or sun-painting—so denominated by said Hill—ask leave to submit the following report:

Mr. Hill having been before the committee, explained to them the history and principles of his invention, and submitted to their inspection numerous specimens of the productions of his art or invention, the committee have formed the opinion that those specimens afford sufficient proofs that the inventor has solved the problem of photographic coloration. The committee had in their hands the plates, unprotected by glass or any other covering, and saw them freely rubbed, and otherwise tested, confirming in their minds the fact of the invention and the durability of the pictures. It is believed that most of the philosophers, both in Europe and America, long since gave up as hopeless the search after this branch of science, which has now been discovered by one of our own citizens, in one of the wild valleys of the Catskill mountains, far removed from the schools of art. The committee learn that Mr. Hill has arrived at this discovery, by which the works of nature may be copied in their original hues, through three years of persevering toils.

The committee are informed by Mr. Hill that his discovery has not yet been perfected in its practical details, which is not surprising, it being but little more than two years since he obtained his first result. But the beauty of the results to which the process has already attained would seem to afford evidence that it will be perfected at no very distant day.

The prospective utility and importance of this invention are very apparent, in its application to portraits, landscapes, botany, morbid anatomy, mineralogy, conchology, aboriginal history, the reproduction of valuable paintings, and to various ornamental purposes.

The committee are satisfied of Mr. Hill's claim to originality and priority of invention, and deem it but just and right that he should be suitably protected and encouraged; and they deem it more particularly so, seeing that a rival claim has been set up in France since the announcement of his discovery was made. The means by which this process is carried out being strictly chemical, it would seem that the existing patent laws would not afford to the inventor the security required. Owing, however, to the short period remaining of the present session of Congress, and the press of business, the committee have been unable to devise any better or more efficient mode by which to recognise the claim of Mr. Hill, than by recommending that his memorial, together with this report, be placed on the records of the Senate.

14. *Humphrey's Journal,* VII (1855), pp. 222, 223. In an article entitled "Retrospective Criticism," the author is possibly referring to the same scene described by Hill (in the text). "Hill's claims far surpass those of Becquerel for 'natural colors' . . . M. Beauregard's being nowhere compared with his, as witness his (H.'s) door-yard mountain 5 miles distant, on the same plate."

15. *Seventh Census of the United States,* 1850, Lexington, Greene County, New York, p. 281. Listed Mary Hill, ten months old.

16. *Scientific American* (March 22, 1851).

17. The following daguerreians are listed as having seen Hill's experiments: J. Gurney, C. C. Harrison, A. Morand, C. W. Meade, and S. Holmes of New York; M. Shew of Philadelphia; C. E. Johnson of Cleveland; C. L'Homdieu of Charleston; R. E. Churchill of Albany. (*The Daguerreian Journal,* 2 [1851], p. 338.) Other distinguished daguerreians who were adherents of Hill include: Lawrence, Root, Whitehurst, Whipple, Richards, Hawkins. Artists of the brush listed were: Harding, Vanderlyn, Waugh of Philadelphia, Hite, Wyeth. (*Humphrey's Journal,* IV [1852], p. 270.)

18. *Putnam's Monthly Magazine,* 1, February, 1853. On page 237 is found an interesting account of experiments with colors including greens. "M. Niépce de St. Victor has lately presented to the French Academy certain specimens of Photography, obtained in colors by a new process of his own discovery. The principle upon which he operates is similar to that propounded by the Rev. L. L. Hill, in this country,—the fixing of the natural colors of objects by means of a plate and camera, in the manner of the daguerreotype. Mr. Hill has not yet produced his specimens, and M. St. Victor finds a radical difficulty in the evanescent character of his works. The colors have all been obtained, and, what is more extraordinary, metallic surfaces are taken with their own characteristics. A great difficulty in the method of taking the pictures, is that of obtaining many colors at once,—bright tints being produced more readily than the darker ones. The worst is the deep green of leaves, while white is quite easy. M. St. Victor further states, that the colors are rendered much more vivid by the use of ammonia."

19. *Humphrey's Journal,* IV (1852), p. 271.

20. There is evidence Hill often posed his daughter either full length or seated on a trunk. See plate 53 of Mary Hill. This daguerreotype in the author's collection also shows other names written on the plate: Hill, S. Morse, Root, and a partial name believed to be Richards; the date 1852 also appears. Of interest, the signature "Root" appears in blue, while the other names are in pale yellow. This is possibly an experimental plate to give validity to Hill's claim.

21. Both the editor of *The Photographic Art Journal* and the editor of the *Scientific American* were leaders in denouncing Hill. Many other publications followed this pattern. Samuel Morse angered by the press wrote in a published letter in the *National Intelligencer,* October 8, 1852: "Mr. Hill has made a great discovery. It is not perfected . . . who has a right to demand him to reveal it to the public now? Who indeed has a right to demand it any time?" It is interesting to note that Henry Hunt Snelling, editor of *The Photographic Art Journal,* was general sales manager for the firm of Edward Anthony, large New York dealers of daguerreotype materials, from 1843–1857. Edward Anthony had tried without success to purchase Hill's process. Interestingly, after Morse had endorsed Hill's invention, the New York operators raised their offer for Hill's process from $50,000 to $100,000. (Beaumont Newhall, *The Daguerreotype in America,* New York: Duell, Sloan and Pearce, 1961, p. 102.)

22. Letter to Levi Hill from Samuel Morse dated October 6, 1852. It was reprinted in *The New York Times* on October 26.

23. *Ibid.*

24. *Ibid.*

25. The daguerreotype continued to be made, but in declining numbers, into the 1860's.

26. Levi L. Hill. *Treatise on Heliochromy* (New York: Robinson and Caswell, 1856), pp. 155–162. Hill's formula is chapter XIV titled *The Hillotype.*

27. A published letter in the *National Intelligencer,* October 8, 1852.

28. *U. S. Letters Patent,* 8,633 (January 6, 1852). The quotation is found in the patent record.

29. *Humphrey's Journal* (1852), p. 88.

CHAPTER 3

1. Josiah B. Millet, *The Life and Works of George Fuller* (Boston and New York: Houghton Mifflin Company, 1886), pp. 14, 15.

2. Beaumont Newhall, p. 154.

3. Robert Taft, pp. 261, 262.

4. Mr. Sam Stevens, town historian of Lebanon, New Hampshire, identified the Lebanon, New Hampshire, scene as the Town Hall. An artist's rendition of the same scene was in an old newspaper clipping of 1890 in Mr. Stevens's collection. The original painting hangs in the town library today. Mr. Stevens had voluminous amounts of old newspapers and town records.

5. *Exposition of 1851 on Industries at Crystal Palace, London,* report (London: 1852), pp. 1440–1470. Number 377 in the United States section of report.

6. *New York Tribune* (October 31, 1853, p. 1, adv.; December 10, 1853, p. 1, adv.); *California Historical Society Quarterly* (v. 6, 1927, pp. 109, 238; v. 6, number 3, September 5, 1927).

7. *Putnam's Monthly Magazine,* 1, February, 1853, p. 121. A footnote at the bottom of this page states: "These papers are illustrated with engravings from daguerreotypes, and drawings with one or two exceptions made expressly for this purpose."

8. Levi L. Hill, pp. 16–17.

CHAPTER 4

1. Graham Reynolds, *English Portrait Miniatures* (London: Adam and Charles Black, 1952), pp. 164, 165.

2. Holograph letter signed M. B. Brady, June, 1843, in which he wrote he was manufacturing jewel cases and often supplied daguerreian operators. This letter is in the Boyer Collection at George Eastman House, Rochester, N. Y.

3. The authors took apart an early case, c. 1840, and the paper-thin leather covering was then soaked in water. Also, several other designs of the 1840's were taken apart and tested in the same manner. It was found that the embossings of these early cases were paper-thin; they were actually leather of chamois quality and not paper varnished and tooled to resemble leather as is commonly supposed. It is true, however, that a great many paper-embossed covers came into use during the 1850's and 1860's, and they are sometimes difficult to detect from the leather-covered cases.

4. Beaumont Newhall, p. 128. A case by Boston casemaker J. H. Smith cost $17 in 1845.

5. A study by the authors reveals about thirty variations in the "Delicate Rose" motif.

6. Notes on Scovill Manufacturing Company, courtesy of Dr. P. W. Bishop.

7. *Ibid.*

8. Henry H. Snelling (1854). In the rear of *A Dictionary of the Photographic Art* there is a catalog of Edward Anthony and Co., daguerreotype material manufacturers. In the introduction pages, vi, vii, viii, there is information on the manufacture of the miniature cases.

9. *U. S. Letters Patent,* 10,465.

10. *U. S. Letters Patent,* 10,953.

11. Henry H. Snelling (1854), Anthony catalog (introduction), pp. vii, viii.

12. *The Daguerreian Journal* (1851), p. 80.

13. *U. S. Letters Patent,* 9,611; *Scientific American* (May 28, 1853).

14. *Humphrey's Journal* (1855), p. 12.

15. *Ibid.* (1852), p. 269.

16. Notes on Scovill Manufacturing Company, courtesy of Dr. P. W. Bishop.

17. *U. S. Letters Patent,* 11,758.

Biographical Notes—Artists and Daguerreians

America, in the era 1840–1860, had a definite intermingling of the established arts and early photography. The following tabulation will prove that this was a factual reality and should illustrate, often, the extent of the interaction of the several arts. Many men, from all walks of life, contributed greatly to the development of daguerreian art. Of necessity, the list has excluded many pioneers in this field of art who might have been influenced by, but are not directly connected with, the established arts of the period. Many omitted were prominent daguerreians.

In compiling this partial list of biographies of qualified daguerreians, it was often necessary to reconcile the existing historical data of art and photography; often, each provided a complementary bit or piece to the other.

Key to Abbreviations

Standard Abbreviation In *Webster's New World Dictionary, College Edition.* Abbreviations for additional sources of research shown below:

BD—Business directory or register for the city and date noted.

BN—Beaumont Newhall, *The Daguerreotype in America,* Duell, Sloan and Pearce, 1961.

CD—City directory or register for the city and date noted.

JL—Jean Lipman, *American Primitive Painting,* Oxford University Press, 1942.

NYC—New York City.

NYHS—George C. Groce and David H. Wallace, *The New-York Historical Society's Dictionary of Artists in America, 1564–1860,* Yale University Press, 1957.

Root—M. A. Root, *The Camera and the Pencil,* 1864.

RT—Robert Taft, *Photography and the American Scene,* The Macmillan Company, 1938.

Barnes, C.
Active as a daguerreian in Mobile, Ala., at 54–58 Dauphin St., 1850–1860. Advertised in 1859: "Photographs made with camera . . . They

are then colored by a regular portrait painter—in oil, water or pastel —any size—miniature to life."
CD; BN.

Bogardus, Abram (Abraham)
Portrait painter and daguerreian. Born Dutchess Co., N. Y., 1822; died Brooklyn, N. Y., 1908. Moved to NYC, 1837; exhibited painting(s) at Amer. Inst., 1845; opened daguerreian gallery at 363 Broadway, NYC, 1846; first president, Natl. Photographic Assoc., 1868–1874.
Root; NYHS; BN.

Boisseau, Alfred
Portrait, genre, landscape painter, art teacher, art dealer, and daguerreian. Born Paris, France, 1823. Exhibited at the Salon (France), 1842. Moved to New Orleans, La., 1845–1846; NYC, 1849 and 1852. Exhibited at Natl. Academy and Amer. Art Union respectively. Advertised as a teacher and painter, Cleveland, O., 1852 (Dec.) and 1853 (Jan.); advertised as a daguerreian at 111 and 113 Superior St., Cleveland, 1855; specialized in taking daguerreotypes with a landscape background. He remained in Cleveland as late as 1859.
NYHS; Cleveland newspaper, 1855.

Bolles, Jessie H.
Artist, daguerreian, and merchant. Owned "Temple of Art Daguerreian Parlor,". King and Liberty sts., Charleston, S. C., 1857–1859. Partner of Wenderoth (1857).
NYHS; CD, 1859.

Bradley, Henry W.
Born Wilmington, N. C. Listed as artist, San Francisco, Calif., 1850. Listed as daguerreotypist, 1852, 1855, 1856 at 117½ Clay St., San Francisco. Later partner of Rulofson.
BN; CD, San Francisco.

Brady, Mathew B.
Daguerreian artist, photographer, and author. Born Warren Co., N. Y., c. 1823; died NYC, 1896. As a young man, he copied sketches for the itinerant artist William Page in upstate N. Y. Page and Brady moved to NYC about 1837. Studied daguerreotyping, 1840–1842; manufactured miniature cases, 1843–1845; opened first daguerreian gallery, 1844 (?); published "Gallery of Illustrious Americans," 1850; exhibited daguerreotypes, World's Fair, London, 1851 (won prize medal).

Most famous for his photographic battlefield scenes of the Civil War.
CD; BD; RT; BN: James D. Horan, *Mathew Brady,* 1955; Josephine Cobb, *Mathew B. Brady's Photographic Gallery in Washington* (booklet), 1955.

BRITT, PETER
Portrait, landscape painter, and daguerreian. Born Mar. 11, 1819, Obstalden (Switzerland); died Oregon, 1909 (?). Came to America, 1843. Settled Highland, Ill., as daguerreian, 1844–1849; itinerant Oregon Terr., 1850–1853; settled Jacksonville, Oregon, 1854; established first daguerreian gallery in the terr. (1854). Displayed his oil portraits and landscapes in gallery.
NYHS; R. Peattie, *The Pacific Coast Range.*

BROWN, ELIPHALET M., JR.
Lithographer, portrait, historical, marine artist, and daguerreian. Born Newburyport, Mass., 1816; died NYC, Jan. 23, 1886. Lithographer used by Currier & Ives, NYC, 1839–1845. Exhibited at Natl. Academy, 1841. E & J Brown, 1846–1848; Brown and Severyn, 1851; Currier & Ives, 1852. Daguerreotypist and artist, Perry's expedition to Japan, 1852–1854.[1] Employed by U.S. Navy, 1855–1875.
NYHS.

BRYANT, HENRY
Portrait, landscape artist, engraver, and daguerreian. Born Manchester Green, E. Hartford, Conn., 1812; died E. Hartford, Dec. 7, 1881. Apprenticed as an engraver, became an itinerant portrait painter, c. 1832. Stayed in Albany, N. Y., 1834–1835; went to NYC (?)–1840. Elected an associate of the Natl. Academy in 1837. Exhibited there (1837–1840) and at the Apollo Assoc. (1838–1839). Learned daguerreotyping Hartford, Conn.; practiced the daguerreian arts in Va. from 1844–1846. About 1850, began to specialize in landscape painting. Exhibited at the Natl. Academy, 1852–1854; made his home in E. Hartford from about 1850.
NYHS.

[1] Brown claimed in his petition to Congress, March 23, 1860 that he had taken over four hundred pictures while on the Perry expedition. Many of these were used to illustrate the Commodore's work on the expedition. Lithographs were made from other daguerreotypes taken by Brown on his trip to Japan. These were subsequently published in other years by Brown or other lithographers. Courtesy of Miss Josephine Cobb.

Canfield, H. D.
Painter and daguerreian. Worked in St. Louis, 1851–1853.
Mo. Historical Society.

Carvalho, Solomon Numes
Portrait and landscape painter, daguerreian and photographer, explorer, inventor. Born Charleston, S. C., 1815; died NYC, 1899. Began drawing charcoal sketches after shipwrecked in West Indies, 1835. Moved to Baltimore, Md., 1828; Phila., 1835. Worked in Charleston and Washington, 1840's. Owned daguerreian gallery at 4th and Pennsylvania, Washington, D. C., and at 205 Baltimore St., Baltimore, Md., 1849. Exhibited at Pa. Academy, Phila., 1849 (paintings). C. 1850, opened daguerreian gallery, Charleston, S. C., 1850–1852. Invented enameled daguerreotype, 1852. Employed by J. Gurney, 1853. Exhibited Maryland Historical Inst., 1850 and 1856 (paintings). Daguerreotypist and artist on Frémont's expedition, 1853–1854. Moved to Baltimore, Md., latter part of 1850's and to NYC, 1860. Listed artist or photographer, NYC, until 1880.
NYHS; BN; RT; CD; the Columbia Historical Society Records, Vols. 53–56 (Cobb).

Chase, Lorenzo G.
Artist and daguerreian. Partner of L. M. Ives, 1844–1846; "Chase's Daguerrian Rooms" at 247 Washington St., Boston, 1846–1851. Listed as artist at 299 Washington St., 1852–1853, and 173 Washington St., Boston, 1854.
Root; CD, 1844–1854.

Clifford, R. A.
Portrait painter and daguerreian, Milwaukee, Wis., 1850's.
NYHS.

Cone, D.D.
Artist and daguerreian. Listed in Fisherville, New Hampshire, 1849.
New Eng. BD.

Cook, George Smith
Artist and daguerreian. Born Stratford, Conn., 1819; died Bel Air, near Richmond, Va., 1902. Began daguerreotyping, c. 1840; traveled as an itinerant, 1840–1844; settled New Orleans and studied painting, c. 1838–1845. Opened daguerreian studio, New Orleans, 1845. Exhibited

five frames at Amer. Inst., Oct., 1846; in Charleston, S. C., 1849–1850. Operated Brady NYC gallery, 1851; listed as a daguerreian at 235 King St., Charleston, S. C., 1852–1875. Exhibited South Carolina Inst., 1851–1852; settled in Richmond, Va., c. 1873–1875.

BN; Cat. of Amer. Inst., Oct., 1846; Humphrey's Journal, IV, 18, 1853; CD, Charleston, 1852–1873; Kocher and Dearstyne, *Shadows in Silver,* 1954.

COOK, (MISS) JANE
Amateur artist and daguerreian. She exhibited drawings and rice paintings at the Amer. Inst. in 1842, 1845, 1846, 1849, 1856; exhibited one India ink portrait and one daguerreotype for painting in 1846. She is listed as a daguerreotypist, 425 Broadway, NYC, 1846. She was probably the daughter of Sarah A. Cook.

NYHS; CD.

CURRIE (CURRY), WILLIAM
Portrait painter and talbotypist. Listed in Phila. directories as Mr. and Mrs. Wm. Currie, talbotypists, 1854–1855. Wm. Curry, portrait painter and Wm. Currie and Co., artists, 1856; Wm. Currie and Co., artists, 1857.

NYHS; CD.

DODGE, EDWARD SAMUEL
Miniature painter and daguerreian. Born July 8, 1816; died Apr. 6, 1857. He worked in NYC, 1836; Poughkeepsie, N. Y., 1837–1842; advertised Richmond, Va., 1844; exhibited miniatures at the Natl. Academy and the Amer. Inst., 1842; daguerreian, Augusta, Ga., 1850–1852; nicknamed by *The Daguerreian Journal,* "Old Veteran accomplished artist and paints miniatures on ivory."

The Daguerreian Journal, Vol. 1, p. 339; NYHS; CD.

DREW, CLEMENT

Marine painter, figurehead carver, photographer, and art dealer. Born Boston or Kingston, Mass., in 1807(?). Drew worked in Boston from 1841–1860. Worked around Gloucester, Mass., 1880's and was said to have been living in Maine as late as 1889.

NYHS.

EDOUART, ALEXANDER
Portrait, landscape painter, photographer. Son of noted silhouettist Auguste Edouart. Born London, Nov. 5, 1818. Educated Edinburgh,

studied art in Italy. Living NYC, 1848–1850; exhibited at Natl. Academy and Amer. Art Union. About 1852 went to Calif.; spent most of life here, except brief trip to Europe about 1859. Painted Calif. landscape but best known as photographer, San Francisco. In 1889 or 1890 moved to Los Angeles where he died 1892.

NYHS.

Fahrenberg, Albert

Portrait painter and associated daguerreian, cigarmaker. Born Cologne, Ger. (1825?). Came to America (NYC), c. 1850. Employed by G. T. Shaw, Louisville, Ky., 1859. Listed (census) portrait painter, Louisville, Ky., 1860.

CD; NYHS.

Faris, Thomas

Artist and daguerreian. Began daguerreotyping in O., c. 1841; partner of E. C. Hawkins on 5th St,, Cincinnati, O., 1843; also listed as portrait painter. Had his own gallery at various addresses, Cincinnati, 1844–1857. Bought Root's Gallery, 363 Broadway, NYC, 1858; Root repossessed the gallery, 1859.

BN; Root; CD, Cincinnati, 1843–1857; BD, NYC, 1858–1859.

Fassett, Samuel Montague

Artist and daguerreian. Married Adele Cornelia Strong, 1851; she was a portrait, miniature and figure painter. Fassett is listed at 131 Lake St., Chicago, 1856; listed as Fassett and Cook, 1857–1858; as Fassett and Cook, 122 S. Clark St., Chicago, 1859–1860; continued listing as photographer to 1863.

NYHS; Chicago Historical Society (*Photographers 1847–1900*); Root.

Fessenden, Benjamin

Artist and daguerreian. Born Westminster, Mass., c. 1809; listed at 17 Hanover St., Boston, 1852 as daguerreian; also listed as artist in Boston during the 1850's.

NYHS; CD.

Field, Erastus Salisbury

Primitive painter, portraits and scenes, daguerreian. Born Leverett, Mass., May 19, 1805; died Sunderland, Mass., 1900. Largely self-taught; studied painting with S. F. B. Morse (3 mo.) in 1824–1825; married Phebe Gilmore, 1831, who also exhibited paintings at the Amer. Inst. NYC. Field lived Hartford, Conn., Monson, Mass., and Palmer, Mass.,

1832–1842; moved to NYC 1842–1848. Took up daguerreotyping while living in New York City in the 1840's. Moved back to Leverett and Palmer, Mass., 1848–1859; then to Sunderland, 1859–1900. Primarily a portrait painter in oils, but most famous for his scenes from classical mythology and Biblical history and for his grandiose, "Historical Monument of the American Republic" (c. 1875 and later). He painted continuously for more than fifty years.

NYHS; JL; Abby Aldrich Rockefeller Folk Art Collection, Williamsburg, Va.

Fuller, George

A.N.A. Portrait, landscape, figure painter, and amateur daguerreian. Born Deerfield, Mass., 1822; died Brookline, Mass., 1884. Bought a daguerreotype camera in Boston in spring of 1840. Took up painting, 1841; returned to Boston, 1842–1847. Studied in NYC, painted portraits in Phila. and some Southern cities, 1847–1859. Went to Europe, 1860. Operated family farm, 1861–1875. Resumed painting, 1875.

NYHS; Josiah B. Millet, *The Life and Works of George Fuller,* 1886, p. 14.

Fuller, John S.

Daguerreian, 1855–1859, Madison, Wis.; combined photography with use of oil and watercolors.

CD; Charles A. Seeley Cat., 1859.

Garlick, Theodatus

Sculptor, wax portraitist, doctor, and daguerreian. Born Middlebury(?), Vt., Mar. 30, 1805; died Bedford, O., Dec. 9, 1884. Blacksmith and stonecutter, Cleveland, O., before 1834. Received medical degree, University of Maryland, 1834; daguerreian at 18 Franklin Bldg., Cleveland, O., 1841. Practiced surgery Youngstown, O., for many years.

NYHS; Cleveland newspaper, 1841.

Gavit, Daniel E.

Engraver and daguerreian. Born c. 1819. Purchased the daguerreian gallery of Anthony, Clark and Co., 247 Broadway, NYC, in 1850; exhibited daguerreotypes at Crystal Palace, London, 1851; gave up daguerreotyping, 1852. Listed Gavit and Co., engraver, NYC, 1859 and Albany, N. Y., 1860's.

NYHS; BN; Scientific American, 1851.

Germon, Washington L.

Engraver, artist, and daguerreian. Listed as an engraver, 1845–1854;

as an artist, 1856–1859. Factual evidence shows he was probably a daguerreian in the early 1850's or before at 189 Chestnut St., Phila.

NYHS; Rinhart Collection, No. 258 SD—138—2.

Goddard, Emerson

Portrait painter and daguerreian. Listed in 1849 at New Woonsocket, Cumberland, Rhode Island.

New Eng. BD.

Griswold, Victor Moreau

Landscape painter, inventor, and daguerreian. Born Worthington, O., Apr. 14, 1819; died Peekskill, N. Y., June 18, 1872. Abandoned study of law early 1840's to take up portrait painting. Studied under William Wolcutt in Columbus, O. Exhibited paintings, Amer. Art Union and Natl. Academy, 1849–1858. Became a daguerreian, Tiffin, O., 1850; moved to Lancaster, O., 1852. Invented and manufactured the Ferrotype (tintype), 1856. Moved to Peekskill, 1861.

NYHS; BN; RT.

Haas, Phillip

Lithographer, publisher, and daguerreian. Lithographer between 1837–1845 with views of Washington, Mt. Vernon, technical prints and portraits. Daguerreian at 289 Broadway, NYC, 1844–1857. Listed as a daguerreian, Washington, D. C., 1849. Awarded a silver medal by the Fair of Amer. Inst., 1846. Exhibited daguerreotypes in NYC, 1853–1854.

NYHS; BN; RT; CD; Columbia Historical Society, Wash., D. C.; Root.

Hacker, Theodore S.

Landscape painter and daguerreian. Between 1860 and 1864, exhibited European and American views at the Pa. Academy.

NYHS.

Hanson, Peter

Landscape painter, tulip authority, and daguerreian. Born Denmark, 1821; died, Brooklyn, N. Y., Feb. 22, 1887. Came to America c. 1847, settled Brooklyn, N. Y. Listed as a daguerreian at 189 Bowery, NYC, 1849, only.

NYHS; NYC, BD.

Harrison, Gabriel

Landscape and portrait painter, actor, daguerreian. Born Phila., Mar.

25, 1818; died Brooklyn, N. Y., Dec. 15, 1902. Moved to NYC, 1822; actor, debut, Washington, D.C., 1838. Learned daguerreotyping in Plumbe's gallery 1841–1843. Employed as daguerreian by Wm. Butler, 1844–1848. Played in Park Theatre NYC, 1845. Owned daguerreian gallery, 1848, NYC. Employed as daguerreian by M. M. Lawrence, NYC, 1849–1852. Moved to Brooklyn, 1848 and opened daguerreian gallery (Brooklyn), 1852. Exhibited in NYC, 1853–1854 (daguerreotypes). Became prominent in dramatic, literary, and artistic circles. The engraved frontispiece in *Leaves of Grass* was copied from a daguerreotype of Walt Whitman done by Harrison.

NYHS; BN.

HAWES, JOSIAH JOHNSON
Portrait and miniature painter, daguerreian, inventor (patents 4,573; 11,304; 13,106). Also author. Born East Sudbury, Mass., 1808; died Crawford Notch, N. H., 1901. Portrait and miniature painter, Boston, 1838–1840. Learned daguerreotyping, 1840. Formed partnership with A. S. Southworth, Boston, Mass., 1844–1861.

NYHS; BN.

HAWES (HOWES), SAMUEL P.
Artist and daguerreian. Worked as portrait, landscape, and miniature painter, Boston, 1829–1833. Moved to Lowell, Mass., 1837–1860. Listed as a daguerreian at 112 Merrimack St., Lowell, Mass., 1849 and 1853. The name appears occasionally as Howes.

NYHS; New Eng. BD, 1849; Mass. State Directory, 1853.

HAWKINS, EZEKIEL C.
Landscape and portrait painter, daguerreian artist, commercial artist. He was said to be working in Baltimore, Md., as early as 1806; as a window-shade painter in Steubenville, Ohio, in 1811; at Wheeling, Va. (now W. Va.), in 1829. A portrait and miniature painter named Hawkins worked in New Orleans, La., 1834. Opened daguerreian rooms with Thomas Faris on 5th St., Cincinnati, O., 1843; daguerreian artist, 1843–1860, Cincinnati, O. Owned daguerreian parlor at Canal and Exchange Place, New Orleans, La., 1846. Said to have perfected the collodion process in photography. Held partnership with other daguerreians in various cities, 1844–1860. Exhibited, NYC Fair, 1853–1854. Brother of Thomas Hawkins.

NYHS; BN; CD; The Daguerreian Journal, 1850–1851.

Hayden, Hiram W.

Diemaker, embosser, inventor, and daguerreian. Diemaker and embosser for Scovill Mfg. Co., Waterbury, Conn., before 1854. Was called the "artist of the village," in 1851; produced three daguerreotype scenes on paper, exhibited in Waterbury, 1851; connected with Holmes, Booth and Hayden, makers of daguerreotype materials, 1854–1858, in NYC and Waterbury. Holder of design patent No. 733, Oct. 9, 1855, for ornamental mats for daguerreotype cases. Designed dies for a thermoplastic daguerreotype case which transcribed into bas-relief a copy of Sir Thomas Lawrence's "The Calmady Children."

Scientific American, Mar. 15, 1851; CD, NYC; BN.

Hewitt, John M.

Miniature painter and daguerreian. Listed as Hewitt and Wolford, miniature painters at 461 Market St., Louisville, Ky., 1845; "Hewitt's Natl. Daguerrean Gallery" at 477 Main St., 1848. Hewitt was probably taught daguerreotyping by T. J. Dabyns who established a chain of daguerreian galleries. The galleries were generally operated in conjunction with an artist.

CD, advertisement, 1845, 1848; Rinhart Collection No. 1021—SD—565—6, (plate #60).

Hill, Levi L.

Baptist minister, author, inventor, chemist, artist, and daguerreian. Born Athens, N. Y., 1816; died NYC, Feb. 7, 1865. Newspaper typesetter, 1828–1830; studied drawing and miniature painting under James McNaughton, ?—1834. Baptist minister, Westkill and Saugerties, N. Y., 1836–1845; published "The Baptist Library" 3v. (1843); itinerant daguerreian, 1845–1847. Experimented in color photography, 1847–1856; published *Treatise on Daguerreotyping,* 1849. Claimed first successful color daguerreotype, 1850. Defended by S. F. B. Morse, 1852; Senate Committee and the Patent Office expressed opinion that Hill had successfully solved the problem of photographic coloration, 1853; published *A Treatise on Heliochromy,* 1856; invented and patented, "Improvement in the Manufacture of Burning-Fluids" (1858); "Hydocarbon-Vapor Apparatus" (1859); "Improvement in Making Illuminating Gas" (1862); "Improvement in Producing Light and Heat and Applying the Same" (1863). Moved to NYC, 1863.

Hill, L. L., *Treatise on Heliochromy,* 1856; The New York Times, Oct. 26, 1852; New York Herald, Feb. 8, 1865, p. 2, col. 4; 32nd

Congress, Rep. Com. No. 427 by Mr. James, Mar. 3, 1853. U. S. Patents, 20,558; 26,497; 35,610; 38,137.

HOPES, CAROLINE
Offered training in drawing and painting in conjunction with daguerreotype portraiture in St. Louis, Mo., 1846.

Charles van Ravenswaay, "The Pioneer Photographers of St. Louis," Bulletin of the Missouri Historical Society, X (October, 1953), 48–71, illus.

HOUGH, EUGENIO K.
Artist and daguerreian. Primitive pastels while working in Vt., c. 1850. Settled in Petersburg, Va., as an artist and daguerreian, 1858.

NYHS; Chas. A. Seeley Cat., 1859.

HOUSEKEEPER, CHENEY H.
Artist and daguerreian. Born Pa., c. 1812. Living * in Phila. in Aug., 1850.

NYHS; Rinhart Collection, daguerreotype No. 38 SD—14—6.

IVES, LOYAL MOSS
Portrait painter and daguerreian. Daguerreian partner of Lorenzo Chase, Boston, 1844–1846. Ives Daguerrian Gallery, 142 Washington St., Boston, 1847–1852; partner of C. H. Callagan, c. 1850. Portrait painter, New Haven, Conn., latter part of 1850's and NYC, c. 1863–1890.

NYHS; Root; CD; The Daguerreian Journal, 1851.

JACOBS, EMIL
Portrait painter, art dealer, and daguerreian. Address, 73 Camp St., New Orleans, La., 1851–1856.

NYHS; CD.

JOHNSON, CHARLES E.
Engraver and daguerreian, listed Superior and Bank sts., Cleveland, O., 1850–1851; partnership Johnson and Fellows, same address, 1851. Probably same Charles E. Johnson, engraver, Spiegle and Johnson, Phila., 1855–1857.

NYHS; Cleveland newspaper, 1851, 1852; The Daguerreian Journal, 1851.

JONES, J. (JOHN)
Artist, daguerreian. Born Maryland, 1802. Probably same J. Jones

* Listed, 159 Chestnut St., Phila. as address c. 1850.

who advertised in 1848 that he had produced an imperishable daguerreotype which could be wiped off with a cloth. Census shows a J. Jones in Baltimore in 1860.

NYHS; Scientific American, 1848.

JONES, J. WESLEY

Artist, lecturer, and daguerreian. Jones and Wm. N. Bartholomew, a drawing teacher from Boston, went to Calif., 1850. Daguerreotyped 1,500 landscape scenes of the Rockies, Calif., and the plains to the Missouri River, 1850–1851. Lectured in Eastern cities, using paintings and sketches made from daguerreotypes, under the lecture title, "The Pantoscope of California," 1853–1854. Paintings sold in lottery, 1854; fate unknown.

NYHS; RT; Rinhart Collection, No. 1166—SD—690—6, J. Wesley Jones, artist.

KELSEY, C.

Portrait painter, daguerreian. Probably the same C. C. Kelsey who opened his daguerreian gallery at 136 Lake St., Chicago, 1848, and was a daguerreian on Lake St. until at least 1858.

NYHS; Chicago Historical Society, *Photographs, 1847–1900;* Ill. State Directories.

KERN, EDWARD MEYER

Landscape, figure studies in watercolor, pencil, and oils, topographer, explorer, daguerreian. Born Phila., Oct. 26, 1823; died Nov. 25, 1863. Exhibited Artist Fund Society, 1841. Topographer on Frémont's third expedition, served under Frémont in Calif. during war with Mexico, 1845–1847; served on Frémont's 4th expedition to the Colorado Rockies, 1848–1849; topographer with Simpson's expedition into Navajo Country, 1849. Daguerreian and artist with the "exploration and survey of the China Seas and Behring Straits of the North Pacific ocean aboard the sloop, 'Vincennes,'" 1853–1854; an official artist of the Ringold exploration of the North Pacific to 1856. Joined U. S. Navy's survey of a route from Calif. to China, 1858–1860.

NYHS; Smithsonian Report, 1854.

KIMBALL, WM. H.

Miniature painter and daguerreian. Born Goffstown, N. H., Apr. 6, 1817; died Concord, N. H., Mar. 10, 1892. Studied miniature painting in Boston; practiced in Manchester, N. H., Lowell, Mass., and Phila. Edited a newspaper, Manchester, N. H., 1842–1844. Began daguerreo-

typing, 1844; listed as a daguerreian at 142 Main St., Concord, N. H., 1849. Served as state librarian of N. H., Concord, 1867–1890.
NYHS; Eastern Dir., 1849.

LION (LYONS), JULES
Portrait, miniature painter, lithographer, and daguerreian. Born France, c. 1816. Came to New Orleans about 1837. Credited to be the first daguerreotypist in New Orleans; listed in directory as "free man of color," 1851. He painted a portrait of John James Audubon.
NYHS.

MASON, WILLIAM G.
Engraver, landscape painter, amateur daguerreian, and agent for daguerreotype apparatus. Began painting or engraving, c. 1822–1860. Mason and Joseph Parker of Philadelphia probably were the first amateur daguerreians in America, 1839. Mason is also credited with taking the first daguerreotype with artificial light; exhibited landscape painting at the Pa. Academy, 1843. Became an agent for E. Whitemaker (daguerreotype plates) at 46 Chestnut St., Phila., 1846.
NYHS; Root; Scientific American, 1845; Eastern Dir., 1846.

MAYR, CHRISTIAN
Portrait, genre painter, designer, daguerreotypist. Born Germany, c. 1805; died NYC, Oct. 19, 1851. First appeared when he exhibited at the Natl. Academy, 1834; went to Boston, 1839; to Charleston, S. C., 1840–1843; visited New Orleans, 1844; returned to home on Lespenard St., NYC, 1845–1851. He was associate of the Natl. Academy 1836–1849 and was elected Academician, 1849.
NYHS.

MINIS, ———
Miniature painter and photographer, Petersburg, Va., 1857
William B. O'Neal, *John Toole,* Univ. of Va. Press.

MORAND, AUGUSTUS H.
Artist and daguerreian. Learned daguerreotyping in 1840; listed as an artist in NYC, 1841. Traveled as a daguerreian in South America in 1842; itinerant in the South, 1844–1845; listed as a daguerreian at 73 Chambers St., NYC, 1846; listed as a daguerreian in St. Louis, Mo., 1847. Returned to NYC at 132 Chatham St., 1858–1859.
BN; Root; BD, 1846–48–49; The Daguerreian Journal, 1851; Chas. A. Seeley Cat., 1859.

MORSE, SAMUEL FINLEY BREESE
Portrait, miniature, historical painter, sculptor, inventor, and daguerreian. Born Charlestown, Mass., Apr. 27, 1791; died in NYC, Apr. 2, 1872. Graduated Yale, 1810. Studied under Washington Allston and Benjamin West in London, 1811–1814. Painted portraits in New England and Charleston, S. C., 1815–?; settled NYC, 1823. One of the founders of the Natl. Academy of Design (1825) and its first president, 1826–1845. Traveled in Europe studying art, 1829–1833; started work on electric telegraph in 1832; first displayed it, 1836; patented it, 1837, and brought it to practical completion, May 24, 1844. Traveled in Europe, 1837–1839; introduced the news of Daguerre's discovery to America, 1839. Opened a daguerreian studio and taught daguerreotyping, 1840–1841; made experiments with telegraphy by submarine cable, 1842. Morse maintained an active interest in arts and science, 1843–1872. Honored by European countries for his invention of the telegraph, 1858.

NYHS; Encyclopaedia Britannica, 1909; BN; Amer. Heritage, Vol. XII, No. 3, 1961.

MOSES, MORRIS
Crayon portraitist and daguerreian, City Hall 30½ E. State St., Trenton, N. J., 1850–1865.

NYHS; CD, State Dir., 1850.

NAHL, HUGO WILHELM ARTHUR
Crayon, charcoal artist, engraver, illustrator, and photographer. Born Cassel, Germany, c. 1820; died San Francisco, Calif., Apr. 1, 1889. Studied Paris, 1848; arrived NYC, 1849; to Calif. gold fields with half brother Charles, c. 1849. Worked as photographer and commercial artist, mid-1850's until late 1860's. Exhibited San Francisco Art. Assoc., 1870's; designer of the Calif. State Seal.

NYHS.

NICHOLSON, JOHN
Portrait, sign painter, and daguerreian. Born Jefferson Co., Ind., July 12, 1825; died Ind., 1893. Worked in Columbus, Ind., 1847; Franklin, Ind., 1850–1860. Later moved to Crawfordville.

NYHS.

PARDEE (PARDE), PHINEAS JR.
Painter and daguerreian. Born Conn., c. 1819. Began daguerreotyping, New Haven, Conn., 1842–1844. Briefly associated as Peck and Pardee, and as Tomlinson and Pardee, 15 Phoenix Bldg., New Haven, 1845.

Listed as an artist, Assembly House Hotel, New Haven, Conn., 1850.

NYHS; Notes on Scovill Mfg. Co. (courtesy of Dr. Philip W. Bishop); CD, 1845.

PERRY, EDWARD (H)
Engraver and daguerreian. Edward Perry, 11 Spruce St., NYC, exhibited wood engraving at the Amer. Inst., 1845; probably same, Perry and Co., daguerreian, 271 Broadway, NYC, 1846–1847; E. H. Perry, Dansville, Vt., 1849; E. H. Perry, 139 Lake St., Chicago, 1854–1855; E. H. Perry, Lancaster, Erie Co., N. Y., 1857.

NYHS; New Eng. BD, 1849; Chicago Historical Society, *Photographers 1847–1900;* Chas. A. Seeley Cat., 1859.

PRUD'HOMME, JOHN FRANCIS EUGENE
Engraver and daguerreian. Born Oct. 4, 1800, Island of St. Thomas, West Indies; died District of Columbia, 1892. Apprenticed to his engraver brother-in-law, Thomas Gimbrede, c. 1814 (?). Noted engraver of portraits and of illustrations for books, 1821–1852. Elected associate of Natl. Academy, 1838; and as Academician, 1846; curator of the Academy, 1845–1852. Listed as a daguerreian at 663 Broadway, NYC, 1851. Banknote designer and engraver, 1852–1869. Employed Bureau of Engraving, Wash., D.C., 1869–1885.

NYHS; Daguerreian Journal, 1851.

REHN, ISAAC
Painter, lithographer, and daguerreian. Painter, Phila., 1845–1848; daguerreian, 1849–1859; lithographer, 1860–?. Displayed ambrotypes at Fair of the Franklin Inst., Jan., 1855. Awarded contract to reproduce drawings of the patent office, 1860 (amount of contract $50,-000).

RT; NYHS; CD.

RICHARDS, FREDERICK DE BOURG
Landscape painter and daguerreian. Listed as a landscape painter NYC, 1844–1845. Became daguerreotypist in Phila., 1848–1866. Advertised could supply daguerreotype copies of "Jenny Lind" in 1851. Gallery at 144 Chestnut St., Phila., c. 1853–1855. A painting, signed by G. W. Merrick, of Daniel Webster was copied from a daguerreotype by Richards. He exhibited views of Pa. before 1856; exhibited several Italian and Welsh scenes after 1856. Exhibited at the Pa. Academy; Amer. Inst.; Amer. Art Union; the Natl. Academy. Took three photographs of President-elect A. Lincoln in front of Independence Hall, Phila., Feb. 22, 1861. To Paris, 1868.

NYHS; BN; Hamilton and Ostendorf, *Lincoln in Photographs,* 1963; Rinhart Collection, No. 847—SD—460—6.

ROBINSON, JOSEPH C.
Painter and daguerreian. Painted a portrait of an old man and an old woman, 1848. Listed as a daguerreian, 170 Broadway, NYC, 1848; listed at 38 W. 4th St., Cincinnati, O., 1850–1851.

NYHS; BD NYC, 1848; CD Cincinnati, O., 1850–1851.

ROGERS, C. T.
Listed at 39½ 4th St., St. Louis, Mo., as a daguerreian, 1854. Possibly the same Rogers who painted the Mississippi River panorama for a production of Uncle Tom's Cabin at the Natl. Theatre, NYC, Mar., 1854. Also a Charles Rogers, scene painter, San Francisco, 1856–1872.

NYHS; Ill. State Dir. (includes Mo.), 1854.

ROOT, MARCUS A.
Artist, author, and daguerreian. Born Granville, O., 1808; died Phila., 1888. Studied painting with Thomas Sully, 1835; teacher of penmanship, ?; began daguerreotyping, c. 1839. Opened daguerreian galleries with partnerships in Mobile, Ala., New Orleans, St. Louis, Phila., 1844–1845; exhibited sixteen frames at the Amer. Inst., NYC, 1846. Opened studio at Franklin and Broadway, NYC, with brother Samuel, 1849–1857. Opened gallery operated by John Clark, Wash., D.C., 1852. Author of *The Camera and the Pencil,* 1864.

BN; Root; Amer. Inst. Cat., Oct., 1846; The Daguerreian Journal, 1850.

RYDER, J. F. (J. M.)
Portrait painter and daguerreian. Born (?); died Cleveland, O., 1904. First listed as an itinerant, 1847. Settled Cleveland, O., 1850; listed as a daguerreian at Superior and Bank sts., Cleveland, 1855–1858; claimed he introduced the ambrotype to Cleveland, 1855. He was a portrait painter in Cleveland, 1860. Introduced negative retouching in America from Germany, 1868.

NYHS; BN; Chas. A. Seeley Cat., 1859; Cleveland newspaper, 1855.

SARONY, NAPOLEON
Lithographer, charcoal portraitist, and photographer. Born Quebec, Canada, 1821; died NYC, 1896. Moved to NYC, 1831. Sold first art assignment, 1840. Employed by Henry Robinson and Nathaniel Currier, c. 1840–1846. Entered partnership Sarony, Major (Henry B.),

and Knapp. Firm did enormous business in lithography, including reproduced copies of daguerreotypes. Sarony was first listed as a daguerreotypist in Yonkers, N. Y., 1857–1858.* Retired from lithography, 1858, and spent six years in travel and art study. Opened photographic gallery NYC, 1864. Photographer NYC, 1864–1896.

NYHS; RT; Chas. A. Seeley Cat., 1859.

SHARP, PHILLIP THOMAS

Lithographer and daguerreian. Born England, 1831. Came to Boston, 1840. Entered partnership with father (Sharp and Son), 1852–1862 as daguerreian. Father was Wm. Sharp, pioneer color lithographer, portrait and landscape painter; Sharp and Son, Chrome-lithographers, Boston, 1852–1853.

NYHS.

SPIELER, WILLIAM F.

Portrait painter and daguerreian, Phila., 1844–1860 and after.

NYHS.

STANCLIFF, J. W.

Marine painter, engraver, daguerreian. Born Chatham, Conn., 1814. Trained as a carriage painter and copperplate engraver. Studied painting with Alexander H. Emmons and Jared B. Flagg; also watercolor painting with Benjamin H. Coe. Listed as a daguerreian, 1849, at corner Main and Pearl sts., Hartford, Conn. Maintained a studio in Hartford many years. In 1878 elected president of the Connecticut School of Design.

NYHS; JL; CD.

STANLEY, JOHN MIX

Portrait and landscape painter, specializing Indian life of Western U.S.; explorer and daguerreian. Born Canandaigua, N. Y., Jan. 17, 1814; died Detroit, Mich., Apr. 10, 1872. Established in Detroit, 1834; made several trips Indian country, including trip up Mississippi, 1858. Lived in Phila., NYC, Wash., and other cities, 1839–1842. Became active daguerreian in Wash., D.C., 1842 (Fay and Stanley). Went to Fort Gibson in Arkansas Territory and West, 1842. Completed a series

* Because of the date (1857) when Sarony was first listed in connection with photography, some doubt exists as to whether he was a daguerreian in the true sense of the word; however, prior to this, he was acquainted with many of the foremost daguerreians of the era. In later days (1864–1896) Sarony became one of the most picturesque figures to appear among American photographers.

of eighty-five scenes in Cincinnati, O., for exhibition, 1845. Accompanied Kearney's military expedition from Santa Fe (N.M.) to Calif., 1846. Worked in Calif. and Oregon, 1847–1848. Sailed to Hawaii, 1850. Exhibited his Indian gallery in several eastern cities and deposited them in the Smithsonian Inst., 1850 (the paintings were lost in the Smithsonian fire of 1865). Went on a government expedition with Isaac I. Stevens to explore a transcontinental R. R. route; took daguerreotypes on this trip, 1853. Lived in Wash., D.C., 1854–1872.

NYHS; BD; RT; Richardson, *Painting in America,* 1956, p. 178.

Stauffer, Jacob

Artist, storekeeper, job printer, pharmacist, lawyer, botanist, and photographer. Lived Richmond (now Mt. Joy), Pa., 1839–1858. Became librarian, Lancaster Athenaeum, Lancaster, Pa., 1858.

NYHS.

Stock, Joseph Whiting

Portrait, landscape painter, and associate daguerreian. Born Springfield, Mass., Jan. 30, 1815; died Springfield, Mass., June 28, 1855. Crippled by an accident at age 11 and spent most of his life in a wheelchair. Began painting c. 1832. Painted mostly Springfield; sometimes New Bedford, Mass., New Haven, Conn., and Warren, Bristol, and Providence, R. I. Diary records 900 portraits painted between 1842 and 1845. Was associated with unknown daguerreian, sometimes between 1840–1855 in Springfield, Mass.

NYHS; E. P. Richardson, *Painting in America,* 1956, p. 208; JL.

Tomlinson, William Augur

Artist and daguerreian. Born Conn., 1819; died NYC, 1862 (?). Partner of the artist Pardee, daguerreian gallery, New Haven, Conn., 1845. Active Poughkeepsie, N. Y., 1846; Troy, N. Y., 1847–1852. Operated gallery at 447 Broadway, NYC, c. 1857–1862. Member of N. Y. State Daguerreian Assoc. on the committee to investigate L. L. Hill's color process, 1851.

NYHS; BN; CD, New Haven, Conn., 1845; Rinhart Collection No. 607—CG—210—6, taken May, 1858.

Troendle, Joseph F.

Artist employed by a firm of photographers in Louisville, Ky., 1859. Possibly the J. F. Troendle who exhibited at Natl. Academy several portraits and landscapes, 1858.

NYHS; CD.

Venino, Francis
Painter, lithographer, and photographer. Active NYC, 1850's. His lithograph of Trumbull's "Surrender of Cornwallis" was published by N. Currier, 1852. Listed as photographer, 1856; as artist, 1858–1859. Exhibited "The Destruction of Carthage" at Natl. Academy, 1858.
NYHS.

Walters, Chas. J. B.
Engraver and photographer. Partner of Benj. W. Tilton at 90 Fulton St., NYC, 1858–1860. Walters and Tilton advertised they took photographs on wood by a patented (?) process in 1859.
NYC, BD; NYHS.

Ward, Charles V.
Landscape painter and daguerreian. Born Bloomfield, N. J. Son of Caleb and brother of Jacob Ward. Exhibited landscapes at the Natl. Academy NYC, 1829, 1830. He and his brother were itinerant daguerreians in South America, working in Santiago, Valparaiso, Chile; La Paz, Bolivia; Lima, Peru; Jamaica and Cuba, 1845–1848. They returned to New Jersey with a small fortune. Possibly the same C. Ward listed in Springfield, Mass., 1853.
NYHS; Mass. State Dir., 1853.

Ward, Jacob C.
Landscape, still-life painter and daguerreian. Born Bloomfield, N. J., 1809; died Bloomfield, N. J., 1891. Began a career as an artist in NYC, c. 1829; exhibited several times at Natl. Academy, Amer. Academy, Apollo Assoc., and Amer. Art. Union, 1829–1852. Painted a view of the scene of the Hamilton–Burr duel at Weehawken, N. J., which was engraved by C. Ward (father), c. 1830. Took daguerreotypes and sketched scenery in Chile, Bolivia, Peru, and Panama with brother Charles, 1845–1847; Jamaica and Cuba, 1847–1848. Exhibited Natl. Academy in London, 1852.
NYHS.

Wenderoth, Fred A.
Artist and photographer, Charleston, S. C. Associated with Jesse Bolles, Temple of Art Gallery, 1857; moved to Phila., 1860.
NYHS; BD.

West, George R.
Topographical artist, lithographer, and daguerreian. Established pioneer daguerreian gallery, Wash., D.C., c. 1842–1850. Assisted William Heine on painting panorama of China and Japan which was

exhibited NYC, 1856. Several paintings exhibited Wash. Art Assoc., 1857. West was commissioned by the Architect of the Capitol to decorate the walls of the old rooms of the Senate Committee on Naval Affairs. Mr. West obliterated his unfinished paintings of historical events because the man in charge showed preference to Italian or French painters to illustrate American history.

NYHS; Josephine Cobb, *Mathew B. Brady's Photographic Gallery in Wash.*, 1955.

WETHERBY (WETHERBEE), ISAAC AUGUSTUS

Portrait and ornamental painter, daguerreian. Born 1819; died 1904. Trained under itinerant painter in Norway, Me., c. 1834. Maintained a studio in Boston, 1835–1846. Went to Kentucky briefly, 1844; moved to Roxbury and Milton, Mass., 1848; opened a daguerreian studio, Iowa City, Iowa, 1854; moved to Rockford, Ill. and began daguerreotyping there 1854–1857; then to Eureka, Iowa, 1857–1859. Finally settled Iowa City, abandoned painting, and remained photographer after 1859.

JL; Richardson, *Painting in America,* p. 258; *Image of America* (Cat.), Library of Congress, 1957, p. 16; NYHS.

WOODBRIDGE, JOHN J.

Artist and daguerreian. Listed as artist NYC, 1848–1849. Also listed as daguerreian at 90 Chatham St., NYC, 1848–1849.

NYHS; CD, 1848–1849.

The following list contains the names of engravers who were also diesinkers associated with designs on daguerreotype case covers.

GOLL (GALL), FREDERICK P.

Diesinker, engraver, and letter cutter. Born Germany. First listed in directory at 112 Fulton St., NYC, 1841–1846 and at 78 Fulton St., NYC, 1847–1860. One of the diesinkers who did work for H. Halvorson and S. Peck, 1854–1860. Also did work for Library of American History, Cincinnati, O., c. 1851. Reproduced in dies, a copy of *The Capture of Major André* from a painting by Asher B. Durand. Other known designs include the Washington Monument, Richmond, Va.; a medallion of George Washington; a horse race; and "The Launching," see plate 83.

NYHS; BN; CD.

Hayden, Hiram W.
See Biographical Notes—Artists and Daguerreians.

Key, Frederick C.
Engraver and diesinker. Was an engraver at 27 Beekman St., NYC, 1844(?)–1849; moved to Phila., 1850–1855. Formed F. C. Key and Sons, diesinkers, at 123 Arch St., Phila., 1856–?. One of the diesinkers who designed cases for S. Peck, 1854–1860 and Scovill Mfg. Co., 1860–?.

NYHS; BD, NYC; CD, Phila.

Paine, R.
Engraver and diesinker. Springfield, Mass., 1850's. Possibly designed first successful die for daguerreotype plastic cases, which was the religious theme "Memorial." This case, probably designed for images of the deceased, is the only one known to be signed by him.

Dr. P. W. Bishop (notes on Scovill Mfg. Co.). Examination by authors shows hinge not re-inforced by metal, but molded in plastic.

Pretlove, David
Engraver, diesinker, and letter cutter. First listed at 241 Cherry St., NYC, 1844–1847, and at 78 Fulton St. (probably partner of F. Goll), 1848–1850. Exhibited engravings, Amer. Inst., Oct., 1846. A known designer of leather case cover designs who signs his name on the die.

CD; BD; Amer. Inst., Cat., 1846–1847.

Schaefer, Anthony
Engraver and diesinker. Listed NYC, 1857–1859. Designed dies for Littlefield, Parsons & Co., (successors to A. P. Critchlow and Co.) 1858–?, depicting historical themes.

BD.

Smith and Hartmann (Frederick B. Smith and Herman Hartmann)
Engravers and diesinkers. Listed in NYC, 122½ Fulton St., 1850–1859; made dies for Littlefield, Parsons & Co., and S. Peck and Co. Designs for plastic cases included reproductions of *Washington Crossing the Delaware,* a painting by Emmanuel Leutze; *The Landing of Columbus,* a painting by John Vanderlyn.

BD; BN; NYHS.

Smith, J.
Engraver and diesinker. Worked for S. Peck and Co. and other plastic case manufacturers, c. 1855–1860. Usually depicted nature, portrait, or conventional designs. Signed his name to several dies.

Rinhart Collection; BN.

Selected Bibliography

American Institute Catalogue. *Exhibition Articles.* October, 1846.

Barker, Virgil. *American Painting.* New York: The Macmillan Company, 1950.

Belknap, Waldron Phoenix, Jr. *American Colonial Painting.* Cambridge, Massachusetts: The Belknap Press of Harvard University Press, 1959.

Cobb, Josephine. *Mathew B. Brady's Photographic Gallery in Washington.* (Reprint from The Columbia Historical Society Records, Vols. 53–56.) Washington, D. C.: 1955.

Daguerreian Journal, The. New York: 1850–1851. Title changed to *Humphrey's Journal.* New York: 1852–1862.

Exposition of 1851 on Industries at Crystal Palace, London (Report). London: 1852.

Fairholt, F. W., F.S.A. *A Dictionary of Terms in Art.* London: Virtue, Hall and Virtue, 1854.

Fairman, Charles E. *Art and Artists of the Capitol of the United States of America.* Washington, D. C.: U. S. Government Printing Office, 1927.

Groce, George C. and Wallace, David H. *The New-York Historical Society's Dictionary of Artists in America 1564–1860.* New Haven: Yale University Press, 1957.

Hill, Levi L. *A Treatise on Heliochromy.* New York: Robinson and Caswell, 1856.

Humphrey, Samuel D. *American Handbook of the Daguerreotype.* New York: 1853.

Larkin, Oliver W. *Art and Life in America.* New York: Holt, Rinehart & Winston, Inc., 1960.

Lawlor, P. J. *Embossing.* Malden, Massachusetts: 1891.

Lipman, Jean. *American Primitive Painting.* New York: Oxford University Press, 1942.

Millet, Josiah B. *The Life and Works of George Fuller.* Boston and New York: Houghton Mifflin Company, 1886.

Munro, Eleanor C. "Portraits in Our Times," *Horizon,* Vol. 1, No. 3 (January, 1959), 95–105.

Newhall, Beaumont. *The Daguerreotype in America.* New York: Duell, Sloan & Pearce, 1961.

Photographic Art Journal, The. New York: 1851–1854. Title changed to *The Photographic and Fine Art Journal.* New York: 1854–1860.

Prime, Samuel I. *The Life of Samuel F. B. Morse*. New York: D. Appleton and Co., 1875.

Putnam's Monthly Magazine. Vol. 1, 1853.

Reynolds, Graham. *English Portrait Miniatures*. London: Adam and Charles Black, 1952.

Richardson, E. P. *Painting in America*. New York: Thomas Y. Crowell Company, 1956.

Root, M. A. *The Camera and the Pencil*. New York: 1864.

Snelling, Henry Hunt. *A Dictionary of the Photographic Art*. New York: 1854.

———. *The History and Practice of the Art of Photography*. New York: G. P. Putnam's, 1849.

Taft, Robert. *Photography and the American Scene*. New York: The Macmillan Company, 1938.

United States Letters Patents. 2,522, March 28, 1842; 2,826, October 1842; 3,085, May 12, 1843; 4,370, January 30, 1846; 4,423, March 14, 1846; 8,633, January 6, 1852; 9,354, October 26, 1852; 10,465, January 31, 1854; 10,953, May 23, 1854; 11,753, October 3, 1854.

Wallace, David H. *See* Groce, George C.

Ward, James. *Historic Ornament, Treatise on Decorative Art and Architectural Ornament*. London: Chapman and Hall, Ltd., 1897, 1909.

Index

All italic figures refer to page numbers on which illustrations appear.